GOT A
SOLUTION?

GOT A SOLUTION?

HR Approaches to **5** **Common** and Persistent Business Problems

Dale J. Dwyer, Ph.D. and Sheri A. Caldwell, Ph.D.

Society for Human Resource Management
Alexandria, Virginia
www.shrm.org

Strategic Human Resource Management India
Mumbai, India
www.shrmindia.org

Society for Human Resource Management
Haidian District Beijing, China
www.shrm.org/cn

This book is published by the Society for Human Resource Management (SHRM®). The
interpretations, conclusions, and recommendations in this book are those of the author and
do not necessarily represent those of the publisher.

Founded in 1948, the Society for Human Resource Management (SHRM) is the world's
largest HR membership organization devoted to human resource management. Representing more than 275,000 members in over 160 countries, the Society is the leading provider
of resources to serve the needs of HR professionals and advance the professional practice
of human resource management. SHRM has more than 575 affiliated chapters within the
United States and subsidiary offices in China, India and United Arab Emirates. Visit us at
shrm.org.

Interior and Cover Design: James V. McGinnis

Library of Congress Cataloging-in-Publication Data

Dwyer, Dale J., 1956-
  Got a solution? : HR approaches to 5 common and persistent business problems / Dale J.
Dwyer, Ph.D. and Sheri A. Caldwell, Ph.D.
       pages cm
  Includes bibliographical references and index.
  ISBN 978-1-58644-366-5
  1. Personnel management. I. Caldwell, Sheri A., 1966- II. Title.
  HF5549.D8763 2014
  658.3--dc23
              2014016021   14-0204

Contents

Preface vii

Acknowledgements x

Chapter 1: Missing the Mark: Why Organizational Problems
Don't Get Solved. 1

Chapter 2: Does This Make Me Look Fat? Analyzing
Organization-Environment Fit. 9

Chapter 3: Common Business Problem #1: Fads, Flubs, and Failures:
How Do We Keep Vision-Focused and Strategy-Directed?. 39

Chapter 4: Common Business Problem #2: Playing to Win or
Playing Not to Lose: How Do We Become More
Competitive in Our Marketplace? 65

Chapter 5: Common Business Problem #3: *Ad Quod Damnum:*
How Do We Deal with All the Changing Laws
and Regulations? 89

Chapter 6: Common Business Problem #4: Extreme Makeover:
How Do We Attract and Retain the Most Competent Talent?. . . . 123

Chapter 7: Common Business Problem #5: Future Shock:
How Do We Deal with a Changing Society?. 157

Chapter 8: Concluding Thoughts. 181

Appendix: Resources and Tips 185

Endnotes 195

Index 205

About the Authors. 214

Additional SHRM-Published Books 216

Preface

This is a book about five universal problems that organizations face in the wake of economic turbulence, realignment of workforce demographics, global competitiveness, and other environmental, cultural, and legal challenges. We do not present extensive theoretical analysis of any of these problems; rather, the purpose of this book is to help you to think through your organization's most pressing issues and then to provide you with ways to address them by using the human capital you employ now or will employ in the future.

We believe that any problem organizations may face can be addressed using what managers claim to be their most important asset—their people. Unfortunately, most managers do not involve their people deeply enough in problem resolution to have a significant effect. Ironically, the very problems that lead managers to decide to downsize, reduce pay, increase employee contributions to insurance, or lock out unionized workers could be addressed, and in many cases resolved, by the very people who are most affected by such decisions.

The benefit of our suggested approach for HR professionals lies in understanding the problems that face their organizations and then devising solutions that senior managers typically will not consider. In essence, human resources can become an even more valuable asset to the organization by using the human capital already present to help solve the problems that keep senior managers up at night. And, of course, senior managers will benefit from reading this book, too, so they can begin to view organizational problems as opportunities to develop and energize employees in managing and solving them.

In the chapters that follow, we show you how to involve employees at all levels in addressing the challenges and problems in your organization. It isn't rocket science, but it does take a completely different mindset and, ultimately, buy-in on the part of your management team. The secret is this: Employees must be made aware of the issues before they become out-of-control problems. In many cases, when managers hold all the organization's secrets, information, and knowledge, but do not share any of these things with employees, they often make wrong decisions that can have deleterious effects on everyone involved. Changing to a mindset that sees employees as a resource to be used for sustainable good is the first step in truly tackling issues that seem overwhelming. This book shows you how to approach organizational problems from a bottom-up, rather than a top-down, perspective.

Organization of the Book

We begin with the notion that most organizational problems are not completely solvable, but require ongoing resolution. The first chapter highlights the approaches typically taken by managers and explains why those approaches do not often work. The second chapter describes the primary four environments that usually pose challenges for organizational adaptation—regulatory, economic, market, and competitive—and explains the misprocessing of critical information in those environments. Moreover, it describes the concepts and processes of identifying the appropriate indicators to assess the problems inherent in the fit between an organization and the four environments.

Each subsequent chapter then takes one organizational problem that has been identified as representing the most pressing ones mentioned by top managers. We determined these problems by surveying CEOs and other senior managers, as well as HR professionals, from for-profit, not-for-profit, and government organizations. Some of our information also came from social media posts on professional group sites, such as LinkedIn. We asked them to respond to the following question:

What are the top three general business/organizational problems, issues, or concerns (do not list individual-level human resource issues) that keep you or your executives up at night?

The answers we received were surprisingly similar, and we grouped them into categories. These categories are represented by the following descriptions:

- Problems that result from an unclear or unrealistic organizational vision and from a lack of well-developed or well-implemented strategies will be presented in Chapter 3.
- Problems that stem from changes in domestic and international competition will be presented in Chapter 4.
- Problems directly related to dealing with federal and state laws and regulations will be presented in Chapter 5.
- Problems that occur because of poor leadership and employee competencies will be presented in Chapter 6.
- Problems that relate to the changing nature of society and the workforce will be presented in Chapter 7.

Following the description of each problem and some selected examples, we present one sample approach to resolving one example problem or issue using HR methods. The sample approach is not meant as the definitive answer. In fact, we hope that the examples we provide spur your own creativity to try something new in your organization. Additional resources, organized around the five common problem areas, are provided in the Appendix.

Most importantly, we hope that as you progress through each chapter, not only will you gain a new perspective on both the problem or issue and the ability to involve your employees as full partners in the organization's future, but you'll also realize you are not alone in having to deal with these persistent business problems.

Acknowledgements

No book is every written alone, and this is no exception. Without the participation of the respondents our problem examples would not have the "real" quality that you see here. We also wish to thank the Society for Human Resource Management for the smooth working relationships we've formed with the editorial and marketing staff. As always, thanks to Kathy Dwyer and Bill Caldwell for their love and continued support in our writing endeavors.

Missing the Mark: Why Organizational Problems Don't Get Solved

"The measure of success is not whether you have a tough problem to deal with, but whether it is the same problem you had last year."

—John Foster Dulles, former secretary of state

One only has to look at the recent headlines or the never-ending television reports on the current condition of U.S. organizations to know that a host of problems confronts all of them. Many of these problems, of course, we blame on the financial crisis, government regulations, and general malaise of our country's political, social, legal, and economic systems that have dominated much of the last 20-plus years. However, though many of the problems have been exacerbated by these systems, most organizational problems have not been *caused* by these external systems. Rather, the responsible parties are generally managers who have missed or misinterpreted crucial environmental information and, as a result, have made decisions that have led their organizations to their current level of instability and, in some extreme cases, eventual demise.

In this book we examine some of the most common problems and issues that organizations have faced in the past few years.

1

Moreover, we take an additional step of proposing resolutions to these problems by using an underused resource—employees. Our basic premise is this: *In times of organizational trouble, making full use of the organization's human capital will save the organization.* As a corollary to this premise, we offer another: *If an organization's employees are not capable of helping an organization in times of organizational trouble, then the management of the organization is to blame for making poor HR decisions (that is, selection, training, evaluation, development, discipline, and termination).*

We realize that these are controversial statements. However, many organizations have found these statements to be true for them. We hope you will discover throughout the book some novel ways to address your organization's problems by making full use of the competitive advantage that your employees provide.

All Organizations Have Critical Problems

Regardless of the perceived level of an organization's success (and by "success" we mean that it is growing, profitable, and outperforming its competitors and that its customers are happy), *all* organizations have problems, many of which go unresolved. In fact, the majority of these problems turn out to be critical predictors of an organization's continuing success or its inevitable decline. What is most concerning, however, is that top managers often do not know how severe the problems are, and some managers are not even aware that critical problems exist in their organizations until it's too late to do much about them.

How can that be? Senior managers are in charge, aren't they? Shouldn't they know what is affecting their organization's success or failure? We believe there are two basic reasons why many senior managers do not see the existence or severity of organizational problems.

First, when an organization is successful, managers believe they are effectively addressing any problems or issues before they become critical. In other words, the mindset here is that if an organization is successful, it must not have critical, unsolved problems. Consequently, the managers believe that they are aware of and in control of those things that affect the firm's success or failure.

Second, managers and employees alike have learned over time to tolerate problems so that they become almost invisible. As a result, the organization has learned to "work around" problems, rather than to tackle them head-on. Think about the last time you heard someone in your organization say something like this about problem X: "Yeah, everybody knows about [problem X], but we don't pay much attention to it; nobody wants to deal with [the red tape, specific person, agency, vendor, central office], because it's just easier to [alternative work-around action or behavior]."

In the first case, managers who believe they control those things that affect the success or failure of their organizations are deluding themselves. Organizations have critical problems primarily because the environment in which they are operating has changed. Although it is certainly true that managers control how they respond to (or adapt to) the environment, they do not control the environment itself. To grasp this realization requires a change in mindset about the extent and type of impact that managers have on their organizations and, more importantly, what role(s) they play in anticipating and addressing critical problems.

In the second case, what has been an invisible problem, or one that has been avoided or tolerated, can become catastrophic when the environment significantly changes. That is to say, an unsolved critical problem is a ticking time bomb that may or may not explode, depending entirely on the extent and type of an environmental change.

All of us have seen this play out in a host of different industries, organizations, and places in the past few years. One recent example was Toyota, which fought to protect its tattered reputation in the United States in public hearings on whether it properly handled recalls and other safety issues surrounding the unintentional acceleration of some of its vehicles. One member of Congress categorized Toyota's approach to unintended acceleration complaints this way: "There was kind of an attempt to sweep everything under the rug, keep it under the table, not tell anybody, and maybe it'll just go away."[1]

Of course, responsible business professionals know that problems don't "just go away" by themselves. In 1982, Johnson and Johnson responded to the cyanide-poisoned Tylenol capsules by immediately removing 31 million bottles of Tylenol products from the shelves, promptly changing the bottle by introducing the first triple-seal, tamper-resistant package, and making presentations to the medical community and to consumer groups to explain the safety changes.[2] The company's swift actions quickly restored lost market share and regained the confidence of consumers and, thereby, was the key to the brand's survival.

The Relationship of Organizations to Their Environments

How critical a problem is depends not on the specific problem or organization, but on how the organization relates to its environment, that is, the organization-environment fit.[3] Whereas a particular organization's problem might be tolerable in one environment, it can be catastrophic in another environment. Hence, the larger the disparity between the fit of an organization with its environment, the more visible and potentially catastrophic an unsolved critical problem becomes. The following environmental aspects are common sources of poor fit:

- Regulatory fit—how well the organization adapts to and complies with laws and regulations.
- Economic fit—how well the organization fits within the larger economy.
- Market fit—how well the organization's products or services suit the market(s) it is pursuing.

- Competitive fit—how effective the organization is in its market compared to its competitors.

The greater the total disparity in all four categories, the poorer the overall fitness level of the organization and the more likely unsolved critical problems will become cataclysmic. For example, if your competitor becomes much more effective than you at improving its services and, subsequently, is able to reduce its prices and increase its margins, this creates pressure on your organization to spend money to become more competitive, thereby reducing your margins and profitability. In this case, the competitive fit of your organization and its environment has become degraded. Likewise, if your organization has high fixed costs, low or inconsistent cash flow, or high debt, these may be tolerable inconveniences in one environment but may become crippling problems in a highly competitive situation, threatening to place your organization in peril.

Degraded fit relationships often emerge unseen by top managers. Companies are sometimes so intent on keeping out the "wolf at the door" they miss the one in "sheep's clothing" sneaking in undetected. By the time the financial impact is strong enough to be noticed, it is often too late to do anything except take drastic measures. Remember—poor fit happens because the environment has changed but the organization hasn't, or the organization has changed but the current environment no longer supports it. Many of the well-known, recent organizational failures occurred because the organization-environment fit worsened, and managers did not address it early enough to avert catastrophe.

For example, consider the situation of the well-known, big box store, Best Buy. At its highpoint, the chain of 2,900 stores accounted for almost one-third of all consumer electronics purchases in the United States.[4] In the ensuing years, however, Best Buy got into grave financial trouble. Early in 2012 the CEO, Brian Dunn, explained its predicament to a group of investors:

Over the last three years, the industry experienced little innovation [in] many of the large traditional consumer electronics categories such as television, PCs, and gaming. At the same time, consumers have enjoyed greater price transparency and ease of costs shopping. As a result, we knew we had to accelerate our cost reduction efforts, adjust our sales mix, and significantly improve on the experience we were delivering for our customers. All of this in the most uncertain consumer and electronic environment we've ever experienced.

The reality is that the cost structure, the sales mix, or the customer service quality was not the culprit here; rather, the technological environment had changed. As Larry Downes noted, "High-speed mobile broadband, cloud computing, tablet devices and the modular nature of app stores have utterly changed not only which products consumers buy, but how they shop for them, upgrade them, service them, and replace them." Best Buy, along with other big box electronic retailers, may not have adapted quickly enough to its changing market and competitive environments.

The Nature of Organizational Problems

Like most things, problems fall along a spectrum. At one extreme are problems that organizations can tolerate indefinitely, albeit they are expensive and time-consuming to tolerate. Examples might be high absenteeism and inventory shrinkage. At the other extreme are problems that cause the decline and eventual death of the organization. Examples of this include having low cash flow with high operational costs or poorly trained employees who produce low-quality goods and services. In the middle are all sorts of variations on these themes.

One of the most misunderstood concepts in addressing problems in organizations is that, given discerning minds and the will-power to do so, all problems can actually be solved. The reality is that most organizational problems require ongoing resolution, rather than one discrete solution. Once a manager understands this, he or she can begin the hard work of managing the resolutions.

In some ways, it is like a patient who has been diagnosed with diabetes. Diabetes is not always a terminal disease; rather, once a patient understands that it is a disease to be managed, rather than one that will be cured, the patient learns to live with the realization that he or she must consider what actions to take *each day* to make life as full and as healthy as possible. There may be no discrete solution (cure) for the patient's diabetes; there is only ongoing management of the problem (disease).

If your organization is like many others, you are probably dealing with problems that seem overwhelming and unsolvable, such as rising costs of health care, energy, material, and labor. If you are convinced that these are "terminal diseases," then you will likely (a) avoid dealing with them until the pain is intolerable; (b) react by blaming someone or something that you perceive to be the source of the malady, such as government regulations, large competitors, overseas suppliers, ambivalent donors, labor unions, or unmotivated employees; or (c) give up entirely. The result of any of these actions is that you begin to perceive your organization as a victim—powerless and at the mercy of others—and this is never helpful or productive in addressing problems.

Avoiding the Victim Mentality

A victim mentality in organizations occurs whenever something external to the person or the organization is blamed for the problems negatively affecting it. In essence, "victims" do not see their own roles in creating or sustaining the problems in their lives.

Furthermore, victims deny responsibility for their actions. They are quick to blame other people and events for anything that has not worked in their situations. As Richard Bach said in his book, *Running from Safety*, "If it's never our fault, we can't take responsibility for it. If we can't take responsibility for it, we'll always be its victim."[5]

Victims are usually angry with the people, entities, or events they think have "done them wrong." Underneath these feelings of anger is almost always the feeling of powerlessness. They are angry because they do not know how to solve the problem and, more importantly, they believe they are all alone in doing so. And, more troubling, victims do not readily ask for help.

Finally, victims lack the resilience to bounce back after experiencing loss or disappointment. They take on a defeatist attitude that carries over to other aspects of their lives and, as we mentioned earlier, this is not helpful because other problems or critical situations may continue to surface.

For organizations, a victim mentality damages employee morale and the overall climate of the organization, and it stifles the will to work on the critical problems. However, understanding the role that organization-environment fit plays in revealing or creating pressing problems is helpful. This understanding permits managers and employees to work *together* on resolving and managing the real problems in their organizations without blaming each other for why they occurred.

Does This Make Me Look Fat? Analyzing Organization-Environment Fit

"The most serious mistakes are not being made as a result of wrong answers. The truly dangerous thing is asking the wrong questions."

—*Peter Drucker, from* **Men, Ideas & Politics**[1]

In the last chapter we discussed why critical problems in organizations usually don't get solved and how they are related to the organization-environment fit. Now it is time to look at information about the fit between the organization and its environments to understand potential problems and their likely effects on the organization.

Before we get into the specifics, it is worthwhile to consider that much of the information needed to analyze an organization's fit with its different environments takes managerial courage to seek out and confront. Sometimes managers feel threatened by information that calls into question their past judgments and decisions. When they feel threatened by such information, they have a tendency to ignore it, discount it, distort it, or avoid it altogether. This, of course, only serves to create additional problems, not the least of which is tension and uncertainty with employees and, later, with other stakeholders such as customers, clients, patients, vendors, suppliers, and shareholders.

The kind of information we are talking about generally indicates some imminent peril for the organization. It may also suggest that unsolved critical problems actually could be resolved *if* the organization could correctly gather and process the necessary information to do so.

And, therein, lies the root of the issue. If organizations are not gathering and analyzing the correct information, or they feel threatened by it, their critical problems will only continue to worsen until they feel powerless to change anything, which begins a downward spiral that usually ends in disaster.

What Is Critical Information?

Critical information is in the eye of the beholder. Information that might be perceived to be critical to a marketing director may not seem at all critical to a plant manager.

However, from a systems-wide perspective, any and all information (such as the following examples from our survey respondents) should be seen as critical cues for indicating potential issues with the organization-environment fit dimensions discussed in Chapter 1. The list that follows contains a few examples from our respondents:

- The quality or price of an organization's products or services is similar to competitors.
- Products or services have a small market share compared to competitors.
- Positive customer service ratings from customers are below 80 percent.
- Litigation or grievances require management's attention most of the year.
- Employee turnover is higher than industry standards.
- Operations are at less than 80 percent efficiency.

We are sure you can think of other examples that would be indicative of a "red flag" to your organization and the fit with your specific external environments. Our point is that unless management hears and correctly interprets this type of information, the problems in the organization will only worsen. Distorting, avoiding, discounting, or misprocessing critical information allows the environment to dictate the organization's fate. When that happens, managerial decisions tend to be reactionary, short-sighted and, often, just plain wrong.

You may recognize this example of a request for a swing pictured in Figure 2.1. In our example, let's say that employees wanted a new incentive system and told their manager what they had in mind. The distortions that occurred, starting with how the manager described what he thought employees wanted through how it was ultimately implemented, created an outcome that was not at all what the employees actually wanted. System-wide, there were several critical essential pieces of information were missing and several steps were skipped, namely asking the appropriate questions and listening carefully to the responses.

How Organizations Typically Approach Problem-Solving

In business schools we teach several ways to solve problems. Many of them require elaborate and time-consuming methods: consensus building, large-scale data collection, statistical analysis, and elaborate mathematical algorithms. However, some methods are far less complex and require only individual or group-level input and judgment.

Managers typically rely on individual or group-level input and then render a judgment based on that input. Generally, this process takes the following approach:

1. The manager is made aware of an issue or problem (for example, declining sales), often by means of a weekly or monthly report.

Figure 2.1

As the Manager requested it.

As Purchasing ordered it.

As Marketing wrote it up.

As the Art Dept. designed it.

As the Supervisor implemented it.

What the Employee really wanted!

2. The manager decides fairly quickly what the problem is or who is to blame (for example, the sales force, a particular member of the sales force, the economy). The manager then meets with the sales force or individual to discuss the issue and come up with a solution.

3. The salespeople provide reasons or justifications for the problem, based on their judgment (such as the territory has lost major customer(s), competitors have lowered their prices, customer service or production departments are not doing their jobs).

4. The manager decides, based on the input from the sales staff, on a solution to use to solve the problem.

Any of these steps sound familiar to you?

There are three important aspects to note about this approach. First, the manager usually receives an outcome indicator (a result) of a problem (for example, declining sales figures), not any predictor indicators or actual data for what the causes of the problem might be. Second, based on the outcome indicator, he or she initially decides the source of the problem (such as the sales force, individual salesperson, general economic conditions) and then uses anecdotal information to come up with a solution. Having little or no objective and verifiable causal data on which to base a decision is often the first mistake managers make.

The third aspect is that the manager makes a decision to employ a particular solution without knowing if the causes are correct. We are not questioning managerial judgment here; rather, the issue is that not having made the correct causal connection in the first place throws off managerial judgment. In other words, one cannot make correct judgments about what to do about a critical problem if one does not know what is truly causing it in the first place.

Here's an example of what we mean. The vice president of retail at a seasonal food distributor struggled with predicting the amount of product to order for each distribution location. Because the majority of the company's sales occur in the fourth quarter of each year, it was imperative to get an accurate estimate of inventory for that period. Despite the VP's best efforts, each year saw an increase in excess product that, inevitably, was marked down after the holidays, causing greater financial loss for the company. The VP, determined to get to the bottom of this problem, pored over the annual buying trends in each of the company's locations. He graphed several years of weather patterns to see whether bad weather was keeping customers inside instead of out shopping. He gathered myriad data and analyzed an abundant number of trends.

What was he missing?

He didn't realize that customers paid attention to the pattern of markdowns and waited to buy the product until after the holidays! The VP was focused on all the things that he thought influenced consumer spending, but the main reason for the problem was that consumers were smart and willing to wait a few days to receive a huge discount on the products. Yet, no one at the firm recognized that it had conditioned its customers into this buying pattern.

Going beyond anecdotal information and actually collecting objective and verifiable data may lead managers to make incorrect causal connections, primarily because they cannot identify the root causes for problems. This happens most often because of the measures or indicator data they use, rather than poor decision-making skills.

What Are Problem Indicators?

There are two types of indicators: leading and lagging. Choosing the wrong one can steer any manager down the wrong path to a solution.

Lagging Indicators

Most organizations rely heavily on lagging indicators. Lagging indicators are outcome measures that help gauge progress or success toward a goal by examining some end result. The use of the term "lagging" reflects a delay or gap between the actions an organization takes and a change in the end result. Lagging indicators are retrospective measures, meaning they tell us what has already happened, but not why it has happened or what to do about it.

For example, if you have ever had your car not start when you went out in the morning to go to work, "failure to start" is a lagging indicator. You obviously know something happened, but you do not yet know what it is or why it occurred. Likewise, if a person dies from heart failure, "a failed heart" is the lagging indicator. Again, the reason the person's heart failed cannot be determined merely by knowing that it did. The government also reports lagging indicators, such as our gross national product (GNP) or the unemployment rate. The causes for growth in U.S. production or for a lot of people to be out of work cannot be explained by knowing only these indicators.

In an organizational context, we also have many lagging indicators: net profit, monthly sales figures, number of clients/patients/customers served (or lost), employee retention rates, crime rates, annual pledges, or donations. In fact, most organizational goals are, at their core, measures of lagging indicators of the firm's success or failure at achieving its vision or mission. The common themes with lagging indicators in organizations are that they (a) tell what has already happened and (b) have a direct bearing on the organization's bottom line (and, thus, presumably provide a business interest in and financial benefit from improvement in the indicator).

If we return to the critical information examples we presented earlier in the chapter, we can see that when each of these happens, each has a direct effect on an organization's profitability:

- The quality or price of an organization's products or services is similar to competitors': Money must be spent to increase quality or quantity of the products or services sold.
- Products or services have a small market share compared to competitors: Need for increased expenditure for marketing resources.
- Positive customer service ratings are below 80 percent: Results in a loss of customers and, therefore, revenue.
- Litigation or grievances require more of management's attention: Money must be spent to resolve the legal or labor disputes.
- Employee turnover is higher than industry standards: Profitability is reduced because of reduced employee productivity and replacement costs.

- Operations are at less than 80 percent efficiency: Profitability is reduced because of wasted capacity, excess resource use, or other inefficiencies.

However, as mentioned before, these indicators, though important for an organization to know, do not help a manager in knowing what went wrong, why it went wrong, or how to improve it. What is needed, instead, are indicators that precede and predict these outcomes—what are known as "leading indicators."

Leading Indicators

Leading indicators are process measures that help managers and employees gauge the incremental progress made toward key outcomes (that is, lagging indicators). They are prospective measures that tell us what will affect the end result or goal at some point in the future. Because leading indicators measure the results from processes, there is less delay between actions taken and a change in the outcome sought.

Remember your car that did not start one morning? If you had paid attention to the sound of the starter (leading indicator) on the previous day, you might have had an indication that it was likely to fail soon. Or, if you had known that your teenager left the interior lights on without the car running for a couple of hours the previous night (leading indicator), you would have anticipated that the battery might not have enough power to start the car the next day. Knowing these leading indicators the day before would have prompted you to take quick action to prevent the lagging indicator—the car not starting the next morning.

In organizations, the critical information that managers really need in order to resolve problems is typically of the leading indicator variety. For example, measures that indicate employee attitudes are poor or that customer satisfaction is low right now may predict future employee turnover or lost sales in a few months. Leading indicators share several common themes: (a) they are the key factors that enable (or prevent) the overall result, (b) they provide immediate feedback on what is happening currently, (c) they provide an early warning of emerging results, and (d) they are responsive to changes made.

The lagging indicator examples used previously, then, need leading indicators that will allow the organization to make changes and then see the consequent results. For example, managers need to know and analyze the causes for low customer service ratings; they need to understand why employees are leaving; they need to pay attention to areas of potential legal liability; they need to identify which factors are crucial in predicting low operational efficiency. Once they understand these things, they can then (a) put measures in place to monitor the leading indicators; (b) make necessary changes to systems, structures, or processes in the organization that affect the leading indicators; and, ultimately, (c) see what happens to the lagging indicators as a result of the changes.

Think of one of the biggest problems for the typical call center—turnover. The average turnover rate for the call center industry as a whole ranges between 30 and 45 percent.[2] In this example, the lagging indicator is turnover. Turnover directly affects the bottom line for organizations through recruiting and training costs, and it also leads to declines in employee morale and overall customer satisfaction. Thus, it is important for organizations to know the leading indicators for predicting and, ultimately, preventing excessive voluntary and involuntary turnover.

Causes of involuntary turnover (that is, employees terminated because they cannot or will not perform well) are often due to a mismatch between the employee's knowledge and skills and the requirements of the position. Some leading indicators for this would include poor hiring and training practices, inadequately defined job expectations, and a lack of resources needed to perform the job.

Causes of voluntary turnover (that is, employees leaving because they are not willing to continue in the employment relationship) are typically attributable to a failure on the part of the organization to meet the employees' needs. Examples for leading indicators of voluntary turnover include lack of career advancement, poor management and supervision, inflexible schedules, insufficient or inequitable rewards, and chronic job stress.

In both types of turnover, knowing the leading indicators or causes can inform organizations about the interventions that might be appropriate to lower the likelihood of turnover. Here are just a few tactical approaches that might work for your organization if turnover seems too high:

- **Make sure that employees understand what the organization values.** This includes aligning the overall organizational strategy with subunit strategies, including customer service, organizational culture, and branding.

   For example, Nordstrom is known for an exemplary customer experience. The focus is on resolution and satisfaction, not on speed or low cost. This helps its staff better focus on what is important to their brand. Going "above and beyond" is the norm. No matter what department you're shopping in at Nordstrom, its customer service strategy is aligned with its organizational strategy. That is its brand.

   Sheri, one of the authors, had a personal experience at Nordstrom when having shoes shipped home from an out-of-state store. The store was about to close for the day. As she left, she asked the sales agent for a recommendation for dinner, which he provided. She chose one of the suggested restaurants across from the store. About 15 minutes later, the sales agent was knocking on the window of the restaurant displaying her driver's license that she had left at the store! Her flight left at 6:00 a.m. the next morning, so there would have been no way to get her license back had the Nordstrom employee not gone out of his way to personally find her and deliver the card to her—and after hours at that. With employees being in sync with the Nordstrom strategy of exemplary customer service, there is a cultural fit and, as a result, the company has one of the lowest turnover rates in retail.

- **Make sure that employees have a realistic preview of their jobs.** At one point in a call center where one of the authors used to work, turnover was close to 30 percent. The hiring managers described the job to the candidates as they were interviewing, but they didn't provide them with actual job descriptions. Once this change was implemented, candidates learned how their roles were to be aligned with the expectations of the department. In addition, they filmed a "day in the life" example to show on the TV in the waiting room, so candidates would get an immediate view of expectations for their position. The managers enhanced the training program and assigned senior representatives to act as mentors. They provided the metrics on which the applicants would be measured up front, so there were no surprises at review time. The applicants had a realistic job preview before they even interviewed, and the job got even clearer as the hiring process continued. As a result, the call center's turnover rate decreased to less than 10 percent within one year.

- **Make sure employees are engaged, not only in their current jobs, but also in their own development.** Employees want to be engaged and challenged in their jobs and careers. However, engagement is often an afterthought for many lower-level employees. Managers first need to understand what employees want out of their job. For example, do they want career advancement, or are they happy where they are? Being content with the status quo is perfectly fine, and every organization needs people like that. Although, if employees want to advance, but no openings are presently available, managers can still offer training to prepare them for that next level.

One organization we know of has an "Emerging Leaders" program. High-potential employees are selected for this program, and the company invests in their growth and development to expand their skills and keep them motivated, recognizing them as the next leaders of the company. The key is to know and understand what each employee wants and is capable of. That not only varies among employees; it varies at different times in their lives. Perhaps an employee who has just had a baby may not currently want the stress of learning a new job; however, in a few years she may be ready to take on such a challenge.

Although it would be nice to know about the relationship between every leading indicator and every lagging indicator, it is just not practical for most organizations to monitor everything. It takes a great deal of time and money to track all the causal connections that could possibly be present in each organization-environment interaction. The key, therefore, is to identify and measure the most critical indicators for each type of organization-environment fit. Next we provide some guidance for making such decisions.

Choosing Appropriate Indicators for Organization-Environment Fit

By now it is probably clear to you that we believe the key to improving the fit between an organization and its environment is to figure out which leading and lagging indicators are the most relevant for each type of environment. This is no small task, but it is crucial to collect relevant information so that you, regardless of your role in the organization, can begin to resolve problems before they become catastrophic. In the following sections, we examine the primary four environments that cause the most concern for organization-environment fit: regulatory, economic, market, and competitive. We also give you examples of each.

Regulatory Fit

Laws and government regulations pervade our personal and commercial lives. Though often criticized and maligned, they are needed to provide the rules and structures for communities, societies, and organizations (both public and private) to properly function. The major concern about regulations and laws—aside from one's political stance or philosophical view—is their cost, which is borne by organizations, their members, and, subsequently, all their stakeholders.

In 2008, organizational compliance with federal regulations cost an average of $8,086 per employee per year— in all sectors of the U.S. economy and across all sizes of organizations. For firms with fewer than 20 employees, the cost was $10,585 per employee per year, whereas it was $7,755 in larger firms (those with more than 500 employees).[3] Notice that costs per employee appear to be at least a third higher in smaller organizations than in larger ones.

The principal driving force behind this differential cost burden is "fixed costs." Fixed costs are those business expenses that do not depend on the size or the productive output of the organization, meaning that these costs would be incurred similarly by a firm with 50 employees and one with 500 employees. As an example, think about two organizations that each own one warehouse. They each lease two forklifts for transporting inventory within it. It does not matter that one brings in annual revenues of $10,000,000 and has 50 employees or that one brings in $100,000,000 annually and has 500 employees. However, in large firms, these fixed costs are spread over larger revenues, higher output, and more employees, resulting in lower costs per unit of output as an organization's size increases. This concept is known as "economies of scale," and its impact provides a comparative cost advantage to large firms over smaller ones.

In regulatory compliance economies of scale play out in the same way. For example, for tax compliance the cost per employee is three times higher in small firms than in large firms,[4] primarily due to the substantial burden of paperwork for the time and resources required for monitoring, record-keeping, reporting, and compliance with statutes and regulations. Safety and health regulations are likewise burdensome because certain regulations must be complied with regardless of size (for example, a restaurant must meet certain cleanliness standards, no matter how large or small it may be). There are many other such examples. That said, from the perspective of an organization of any size, laws and regulations cost money that could be used otherwise for investments and operations.

The Effects of Poor Organization-Regulatory Fit

Remember we said that the larger the disparity between the fit of an organization and its environment, the more visible and potentially destructive an unsolved critical problem becomes? From a regulatory fit perspective, problems become catastrophic when organizations cannot adapt quickly to changes in legislation and government regulations. As a result, they become overburdened with costs, unresponsive to market needs, and, ultimately, plagued with inefficiency and ineffectiveness.

Consider ISS, a small company that manufactures surgical systems that use 3-D computer imaging and robotic tools. In response to well-publicized problems with medical devices, the U.S. Food and Drug Administration (FDA) introduced more stringent regulations that significantly slowed the rate of reviewing and approving new products. Because of increased FDA regulations on medical devices, bringing a new product to market now takes ISS twice as long as it once did, thus increasing its costs for each product (which, in turn, increases the cost for buyers or reduces the company's net profit), and slowing its market responsiveness.[5]

Conversely, airlines were deregulated in the 1970s to remove government regulation over fares, routes, and market entry. Deregulation led to an increased number of regional airlines, surges in fuel costs, price cuts from lower-priced competitors, and a reduction in the number of scheduled flights. Interestingly, the change in the regulatory environment for the airlines was no less problematic than for ISS; both regulatory changes caused a degraded fit between how the organizations operated and their regulatory environments. Neither the small medical manufacturer nor the large airlines adapted quickly to the regulatory changes they faced and, subsequently, experienced several operational and financial problems that still have not been completely resolved.

The question ultimately becomes, "How does an organization improve its regulatory fit?" The answer, as you might expect, is quite complex. Because organizations do not control the imposition of laws and regulations (except through lobbying or more questionable practices), the only option is through adaptation. Understandably, the first step is correctly interpreting the upcoming laws or regulations for the specific organizational context and then looking at the appropriate leading and lagging indicators.

As an example, let's look at a law with which most organizations continue to struggle: the Family and Medical Leave Act (FMLA). The law provides eligible employees of covered employers (that is, all public employers, as well as private employers with 50 or more employees) the opportunity to take unpaid, job-protected leave for specified family and medical reasons. In summary, eligible employees are entitled to 12 workweeks of unpaid leave in a 12-month period for the following:

- The birth of a child and to care for the newborn child within one year of birth.

- The placement with the employee of a child for adoption or foster care and to care for the newly placed child within one year of placement.
- To care for the employee's spouse, child, or parent who has a serious health condition.
- A serious health condition that makes the employee unable to perform the essential functions of his or her job.

Further, the FMLA was amended to provide expanded leave to eligible employees who are the spouse, son, daughter, parent, or next-of-kin of a member of the armed services (National Guard, reserves, or regular armed forces) who have a serious injury or illness incurred in the line of duty. The amendment allows the covered employee to take up to 26 workweeks of FMLA leave during a single 12-month period to care for his or her family member (referred to as "military caregiver leave"). The amended FMLA also added a special military family leave entitlement to allow eligible employees whose spouse, child, or parent is called up for active duty in the National Guard or reserves to take up to 12 workweeks of FMLA leave for qualifying exigencies related to the call-up of their family member (referred to as "qualifying exigency leave").

There are a number of ways FMLA leave can be requested and used by an employee, and it continues to be a source of frustration for many organizations because of the variety of ways it can be interpreted and applied. What is most problematic, however, is that employers are not able to predict with any accuracy the FMLA-eligible absences of valuable and needed employees. In other words, the law itself is not the problem; the problem is in how an organization adapts to it.

This uncertainty causes many organizations to adapt by overstaffing or increasing the overtime allotment so that, on any given day, there will be enough workers to potentially cover those employees who may request or are actually using FLMA leave. Additionally, the organization may adapt by increasing the number of HR staff to handle all the paperwork and monitoring required to ensure the integrity of the leave. The greater the costs incurred due to FMLA regulations, the poorer the fit the organization has with its legal and regulatory environment.

If an organization pays attention to percent of employees on FMLA leave as a leading indicator, then the lagging indicator (number of additional employees needed or number of additional overtime hours requested) will be difficult to predict. As a result, the organization will likely budget for too many or too few additional employees or too much or too little overtime compensation. However, if the organization instead focuses on productivity as its lagging indicator, then actual labor costs could likely remain the same or possibly decrease—even with employees on leave or having to pay additional overtime.

How can that be?

It has to do with how labor costs are calculated. Part of the calculation involves how much money the organization actually spends on wages and benefits. Most managers focus exclusively on this indicator, which is why we have seen the aggressive downsizing, pay reductions, and cost shifting that have occurred in recent years. However, compensation costs are only one part of the labor cost equation. The other part involves employee productivity—how much employees actually produce for that given amount of money. Therefore, true labor costs are equal to pay divided by productivity. In other words, if wages increase (such as through increased number of employees or amount of overtime hours), labor costs do not have to go up *if* productivity also increases.

So, if an organization wishes to resolve its cost concern with the FMLA requirements imposed on it and, thus, adapt the organization to better fit within this part of its regulatory environment, it might choose to focus on the factors of productivity, which it can predict and influence with some degree of accuracy, rather than on the causes and number of FMLA leaves, which it cannot predict at all. Ultimately, individual organizations and their managers have to fully understand what makes the most sense for them. But choosing the correct leading and lagging indicators can provide the critical information they need in order to focus on taking action and making appropriate and effective changes to adapt to the plethora of laws and regulations that continue to be imposed at both the state and federal levels.

Economic Fit

Almost every organization in recent years has likely experienced some turbulence as a result of the financial crisis. Whether you are a member of a for-profit or a not-for-profit organization does not matter; all sectors of the U.S. economy have been struggling in the past few years to figure out how their organizations can adapt to and make the most of a struggling economy.

Many of the issues surrounding an organization's fit with the economic environment have to do with its ability to minimize costs and maximize revenue. Part of the key to this is to be able to predict the costs and sources of revenue that will make the biggest difference in an economic downturn (or upturn, for that matter). Once again, the ability to understand the leading and lagging indicators for an individual organization's economic health is crucial.

We have become painfully aware of the lagging indicators of a global financial crisis: plummeting housing prices that have led to foreclosures, lower returns on financial instruments that have led to practically worthless retirement accounts (and, occasionally, imminent default of whole nations), increased borrowing requirements that have led to lower capital investments . . . we could go on with more examples. As the most recent crisis formed, the leading indicators were not as clear or, at least, no one was paying close enough attention to them.

For example, a *Wall Street Journal* story reported that the orders for durable goods dropped 8.3 percent in October 2006.[6]

Durable goods are the long-lasting and more expensive items, such as computer equipment and industrial machinery, that organizations buy when they feel confident about the economy and their investment in the future. When they are not as confident, they put off buying durable goods until conditions improve. Therefore, "orders for durable goods" is considered to be a leading indicator that predicts whether the economy seems to be getting better or worse. Increased orders for durable goods mean increased production, and that translates into lower unemployment, which leads to more consumer confidence . . . you get the picture. Recently, new orders for manufactured durable goods have increased steadily, which bodes well as a leading indicator for our continuing economic recovery.[7]

Organizations that are tied to manufacturing generally rely heavily on how many orders for durable goods they are receiving. The problem comes when orders begin to decrease but managers' eternal hopefulness that "things will get better next month" does not materialize—over and over again. The misprocessing of such critical information becomes the culprit for what happens later.

Sometimes, however, missing the mark on what the leading indicators actually are is an even more grievous error. Take the case of Toll Brothers, one of the most prominent luxury home-builders in the nation. Robert Toll, the CEO, ultimately blamed the media for the company's recent financial losses. Toll did not seem too worried about home prices when they were soaring to unreasonable levels. In fact, he speculated that the rise would continue. Here's what he said:

According to two recent major studies, demand for new homes is projected to expand in the next 10 years; yet increasingly complex approval processes are constraining the supply of buildable lots. With affluent households—those earning $100,000 or more—growing six times faster than the population in general, we believe demand for luxury homes will accelerate. We now own or control approximately 60,000 home sites, a five- to six-year supply based on our current pace of growth. We believe this positions us to prosper in the coming years from the growing imbalance between demand and supply.[8]

It turns out that there *was* a "growing imbalance between demand and supply" approaching. He got just one thing wrong: It was the supply that was too big, not the demand. Because the CEO was not paying attention to the right indicators, the volatility during the housing boom-and-bust nearly devastated the company.

One of the hardest-hit segments in the economic environment of late has been not-for-profits, which include charities, schools, churches, and advocacy/service organizations, and local and state government agencies. Clearly, most of the challenges here have to do with the scarcity of economic resources that, in these sectors, are primarily due to decreased individual giving, a lowered tax base in their locations, and federal and state funding cuts. Not-for-profits and governmental agencies, by their very nature, are at the mercy and whim of their funders: individuals, government, and, to a lesser degree, for-profit organizations. Moreover, not-for-profits (by law and by custom) do not distribute their surplus funds, if any, to those who own or control them and, thus, are constrained to use the funds they do receive as investments that are poured back into the enterprise to support its mission.

From an organization-economic fit perspective, not-for-profit and government organizations will experience a poor fit primarily when the economy is weak, that is, when people are out of work and their discretionary income is reduced or when the government has reduced grants, funding, and contract availability. Of course, all of these are still in play, and these types of organizations continue to be economically strained.

Identifying the leading and lagging indicators for a not-for-profit organization is just as crucial as it is for a profit-centered firm. Remember: The not-for-profit designation is an Internal Revenue Service (IRS) tax issue, not a goal! Not-for-profits still want to have at least some monetary surplus at the end of their fiscal year. Therefore, assessing the likely indicators that will provide critical information now to inform their decisions about the future will help determine whether their organizations can be sustained through rough economic times.

Recently, Goodwill Industries of Northwest Ohio adopted this approach. The mission of the organization is "We improve the lives of people with disabilities or other disadvantages through employment training and job placement opportunities." All of their revenue-generating activities (retail stores, janitorial contracts, their online ShopGoodwill website, auto auction, and computer recycling, as well as fund-raising activities) are designed to provide the resources to support the mission. As the economy worsened in 2008, the agency's costs continued to exceed its revenue, resulting in a huge deficit. The senior management team began to analyze the crucial predictors (that is, leading indicators) so that they could focus their decision-making on forming solutions before their position became untenable. Because retail is the organization's primary revenue source, they began there.

Following an extensive analysis, they chose several key leading indicators (for example, sales per square foot, staff training, donor count) and several key lagging indicators (for example, revenue, staff retention) and proceeded to track these on a monthly basis. As a result they were able to have immediate, real-time information that helped them see the trends that affect the operation and economic health of the agency. And, more importantly, they have been able to process that information quickly, making decisions that allowed them to end with several consecutive years with substantial surplus funds.[9]

The bottom line with respect to organization-economic fit is that all managers, whether they work in a for-profit or a not-for-profit organization, must develop a thorough understanding of the actions that produce revenue and those that constrain it. Only then will they be able to correctly process the critical information that will determine how well they adapt their organizations to the economic reality of their situations.

Market Fit

How well an organization's products or services suit the market it operates within is the basic premise of organization-market environment fit.[10] Over the years, many products have caught the public's attention, had a tremendous run of success, and then just faded into the sunset, only to be replaced by other trendy products. Beanie Babies, pet rocks, and Hummers are a few well-known examples.

To be perfectly clear, we need to define what we are talking about when we talk about market fit. First, recognize that the term "market" includes both an orientation toward customers ("customer orientation") and toward competitors ("competitor orientation") that exists within a larger context.[11] For our purposes here we are confining our discussion to the notion of customer orientation, as we will deal with several aspects of the organization's competitive market fit in Chapter 4. Moreover, we make a distinction between an organization's response to expressed customer demands and preferences ("reactive response") and building a market to capture potential customers' needs that are, as yet, unexpressed ("proactive response"). The distinction is relevant as we look at the ways organizations improve their fit within markets.

Once again, the leading and lagging indicators are an important aspect of determining just what customer needs are now and what they might become in the future. As an example, consider Kodak, the photographic products giant. Kodak was a leader in convenient and cutting-edge cameras and films for many decades. However, the company lost millions of dollars in the early years of the 21st century and decided to discontinue making cameras.

Why? What happened?

Marketing experts would likely argue that Kodak's timing was off with the changing market, and, therefore, the products did not satisfy customers' needs; thus, Kodak misprocessed market information. Kodak had traditionally sold cameras at a low cost, and film was the primary source of Kodak's growth and profits.[12] The business became heavily dependent on this highly profitable margin from film, and progressively paid less attention to equipment. In the 1980s, Kodak failed to respond to the imminent market change to digital photography. Instead, Kodak's CEO and other decision-makers virtually committed corporate suicide by sticking to a model that was no longer valid in the post-digital age. Kodak could have addressed this change by gradually adapting the business strategy. However, the failure to recognize the leading indicators of a changing market and customer demands has resulted in bankruptcy and layoffs of more than 47,000 workers. The irony here is that Kodak pioneered digital-imaging technology![13]

Although huge organizations like Kodak can afford to spend a lot of money on market studies, it is not necessary for smaller organizations to make such a heavy financial commitment. There are plenty of leading indicators of customer shifts and preferences that occur daily if we would only pay attention to them. For example, many organizations—large and small—now have a presence on Facebook, Twitter, Foursquare, LinkedIn, Pinterest, and other social media sites. However, these sites are often unmonitored or have sporadic postings or updates. Yet, many media experts suggest that customer comments and questions posted on social media sites can indicate subtle changes to their preferences and demands.

For example, restaurant owners in failing restaurants often do not understand why customers are not coming to their restaurants. However, there are often a number of online customer reviews that comment negatively (and positively) on the decor, the food, and the service. Though these postings are readily available to the owners, they never look at them. But their potential customers do.

Your organization, no matter what product or service it provides, can easily take advantage of this type of information *if* you know how and commit the time to evaluate it. Monitoring the products and services customers do not like is just as important as monitoring the ones they do like. Understanding what is wrong with things today, however, is different from figuring out what might be preferred in the future. If you are new to social media, we suggest that you check out "Social Media for Business—A Beginners Guide"[14] and get started today to understand how to harness its power and scope for your organization!

The bottom line with organization-market fit is to identify the most important indicators of your customer/client needs, demands, and preferences, both now and what might be unexpressed future ones. Here are a few questions to ask to determine what is going on with your customers and, ultimately, with your products and services:

1. What are the products and services we offered five years ago (or any recent time frame) that are no longer in demand? When you discover what these might be, ask why. Once you analyze the changes and their reasons, you will start getting a sense of the nature of your customers and how they may be changing.

2. What are we seeing right now that indicates customers or clients are really happy (or really unhappy) with our products and services? What are the keywords and phrases our customers use to describe us? How do we validate what we're seeing? Facing reality, even if it is somewhat painful or minimally informative at the moment, will help develop your organization's capacity and the will to deal with a problem while it is still solvable.

3. What, if we could accomplish it, would fundamentally change the way our customers and clients see us and our

products or services? These are meaningful leading indicators that are often right in front of us, but we don't always recognize them, or we choose to ignore them as a "minority opinion." In making sure your organization fits its market, realize there are never unimportant minority opinions.

4. How do our products and services match the social and cultural changes occurring in our markets? How do we get ahead of some of those changes to capture the, as yet, unexpressed needs? For example, people are having children later in life. What might they need (as employees and as customers) that they may not have expressed yet?

Minimizing the differences between your organization and its approach to customer demands and preferences, as well as the products and services you offer, takes some attention to subtle changes that occur every day. Managers' attention to social, cultural, political, and other leading indicators is crucial for ensuring that their organization-market fit does not spiral out of control.

Competitive Fit

Mary Anne Devanna and Noel Tichy summarized one of the major issues in achieving a competitive advantage that is still true today.[15] They wrote,

By the end of the 1980s we understood that successful companies did not just sell what they made; they made what customers wanted and they made it faster, with better quality and frequently at a lower price. Thus, speed and not size seemed to bestow competitive advantage in the global marketplace. . . . Understanding . . . the challenges in the marketplace and the strategy to deal with those challenges . . . provides the context in which decisions can be made at all levels of the organization.

As we look at the issue of organization-competitive fit, we need to keep several of these challenges in mind.

First, as we noted in the previous section, there are a number of ways to achieve competitive advantage in the markets your organization serves: Speed, flexibility, cost, quality, and timing are some of the more obvious ones. Not all of them may be the most relevant to your organization, but at least some of them should be.

Second, *how* you approach these factors is just as consequential as which ones you focus on. Consider two organizations that both sell lawnmowers. The first one sells two brands—an inexpensive, basic one and one that is considered the top of the line and has a high price. The second organization sells several brands that fall all along the price and quality continua. Each of these organizations competes with the other for market share. If you were in the market for a lawnmower, which organization would you choose to patronize?

Your answer is likely dependent on more than just cost or variety. It probably also matters to you the services they provide after the sale, the speed with which the mower is ready after servicing, the integrity and reputation of the organization with regard to perceived customer satisfaction, the location of the store and, perhaps, other considerations. Our point is that many managers wrongfully assume that they compete primarily on cost and quality. As a result of this assumption, they neglect things that they should really be focusing on and instead focus on things that do not have as much direct effect on important outcomes. Our previous discussion on the issue of labor costs is one such example.

In addition to focusing on the wrong things, sometimes organizations focus on too many things. For example, a consumer products company was sold to a private equity group, and a new CEO was brought in. Like many new leaders he wanted to create his own legacy, and, as a result, he decided to start changing everything. The management team had protracted arguments over procedures, timing, and who future decision-makers should be, not to mention which investments should be chosen.

The new CEO decided to eliminate the annual strategic planning session in which the management team came together to discuss which ideas, projects, and strategies they would pursue. In this forum they agreed on how they would evaluate the ideas, and they determined who would lead each initiative and give progress reports. Once the CEO cancelled the strategic planning session, the management team was unfocused, no longer collaborated, and made seemingly random decisions. Needless to say, the managers neglected the things they really should have been focusing on and, instead, ended up not collaborating on anything. As a result the organization focused on too many disparate things that did not affect the bottom line.

For managers, understanding the primary aspects that influence their organization's competitive advantage is the first step in choosing how they will compete. This is fundamentally a strategic decision. But, more importantly, managers need to know the subtle influences that indicate whether the organization is even able to compete effectively in a particular market. Surprisingly (or perhaps, not so surprisingly), these influences have more to do with intangible factors, like employee and managerial competency, trust, and attitude.

If we assume for most organizations that costs, revenue, and profits are important end results (lagging indicators), then understanding what influences them (leading indicators) becomes the key to being competitive. However, managers need to pay attention to several relationships as they discover what is crucial in their organizations. There is no "right" answer here, but the following questions will help illuminate the indicators of true competitive advantage for your organization:

- What is the relationship between managers and employees? Is it one of trust or one of mistrust? How do we know which it is, and, importantly, if we don't know, how do we find out? This does not mean doing an attitude survey; those are rarely acted on and, as such, are basically useless. What it means is having honest, crucial conversations with all parties to discover the subtleties that underlie relationships in the organization. Analyzing the relationship between managers and their employees is a valuable step that many managers avoid, primarily because they do not want to have to deal with unpleasantness. But, as we said earlier, avoiding or distorting information will come back to haunt managers later on.

- Further, what are the key factors that influence whether our employees trust us and whether we trust our employees? They are predictors of employee behaviors and attitudes and, as such, must be dealt with honestly and openly.

- Have we skimped or cut back on investing in our employees' competency and trust? If so, what will it take to regain or establish them? This is no small matter. Organizations that are not competitive are generally the ones that have minimized the importance of having competent, trusting, and trustworthy employees. There is no more significant investment, and any manager who thinks otherwise will not be in business for the long haul. And we do not mean just paying lip service here; we mean really doing it!

- What is our reputation with our employees and potential applicants? There is a lot of buzz about employment branding, but how much do your managers really know and understand about what that ultimately means to the organization's overall reputation, both in the marketplace for their goods and services and in the marketplace for potential employees?

- How competent, credible, and inspiring are managers? Nothing can kill an organization's competitiveness faster than managers who are incompetent and uninspiring.

Again, facing that harsh reality is painful but necessary for all organizations that wish to truly be competitive.

As you probe more deeply into these and other questions, you will discover that competitive advantage begins with the issue of competency and trust among the organization's members. It is fundamental to resolving and managing *all* organizational problems.

Common Business Problem #1: Fads, Flubs, and Failures: How Do We Keep Vision-Focused and Strategy-Directed?

"Fit no stereotypes. Don't chase the latest management fads. The situation dictates which approach best accomplishes the team's mission."

—Colin Powell, retired general, U.S. Army

Respondents from our survey indicated that keeping the vision and strategy front and center was one of the top problems faced by their organizations. As we read some of the comments and explanations, we realized that most executives perceive many external opportunities and threats, but their failure to decide which direction to take and to adequately plan for that direction make management a reactive—even schizophrenic—activity. We also noted that many of the respondents saw that the creation of a generic or unrealistic vision hampered everyone's motivation to work to achieve it. The basic problem here was aptly summarized by one respondent: "Our most nagging problem is how to keep associates focused on key business objectives. The urgent driving out the most important."

The Roles of Vision and Strategy

All successful organizations have realized that they need to understand what they are in business to accomplish and to devise a means of accomplishing it. In fact, many organizations, whether they are successful or not, have identified a mission, have painted a clear vision, and have developed a strategy. Unfortunately, just having it written down in a large binder does not guarantee success. The key to keeping vision-focused and strategy-directed has everything to do with strategy conception and strategy execution, and this requires engagement by the entire enterprise—including all managers *and* all employees.

We recently heard a colleague describe an organization whose president did not think it was important to share the business strategy with his employees. He believed that because he had only entry-level people, they would not "get it." Unfortunately for this top executive, he missed the pivotal role that these employees play. Equally as troubling, it seems he is not alone in his views.

A Cognos/Palladium Group study reported that 95 percent of managers do not share the company strategy with their employees, and 85 percent of executive teams spend less than one hour each month discussing and executing their organization's strategy.[1] Thus, people working in these organizations have no way to determine whether their daily activities are helping the company carry out its strategy—if they even know what it is at all. Moreover, if top managers do not use the strategy as the criterion for operational activities, the entire organization loses sight of the relevance of daily operations. Keep this point in mind: When employees are engaged on the front line with the issues that are often the harbinger of future problems, they can offer vital information about leading indicators of degrading organization-environment fit. Moreover, organizations that share their strategy with their employees get far greater alignment with their vision and mission.

Sharing also makes strategy execution and implementation much clearer and easier for everyone concerned.

Consider this example. A retail establishment ordered hundreds of backpacks in July in preparation for back-to-school shoppers. Senior management decided to reward the sales associates with $5 for every backpack sold to deplete the inventory by September 1st to allow for a new line of backpacks to be delivered in time for Christmas shopping. To the surprise of management, the backpacks did not sell at the rate expected. A top manager visited the store and expressed shock that the $5 incentive for every bag sold was not working. When he met with the sales staff members to find out why, they explained that they were not told about the $5 incentive, and said that they would immediately begin to push the backpacks. As a result, they made it a part of their standard closing at the cash register, and they even started wearing them in the store. Customers noticed them and asked questions. Within one month, they depleted their inventory and had to place another order.

Employees became engaged. The store employees' vision became aligned with management's vision. They even shared with management that the top-selling bag was black, as that was the "in" color and easier to sell, so that when the new order was placed they should request more black bags. Management began to collaborate with the staff before placing orders for several products, given that the staff members knew their customers and knew what would sell.

Basic Problems with Organizational Strategic Planning and Implementation

Strategic planning involves three activities: evaluating the past, understanding the present, and preparing for the future. Planning is a time-consuming and energy-expending process for the leadership team, as well as for operational managers and their employees. In fact, such extensive planning is sometimes viewed as too costly for organizations, and, therefore, some companies have decided it is not worth it. This is a huge mistake for a number of reasons, not the least of which is that it assumes that the organization cannot or will not control its own destiny.

We believe, however, that a large part of the problem with visioning and strategic planning, in addition to the time and energy required, is that it is often done as an independent exercise, rather than as an interdependent process. In other words, strategic planning is often not undertaken as a continuous and cyclical process, and that is where its fundamental problems begin. Miguel Pina e Cunha and his colleagues have written that strategic planning should be "changing from a detached, analytical, prediction-oriented endeavor, to a dynamic process that combines a vision of the future . . . and a combination of top-down and bottom-up processes."[2] In other words, strategic planning needs to be continual and dynamic and involve members of the entire organization. As noted, strategic planning is not one process, but a *system* of interdependent processes:

1. First and foremost, strategic planning is a *learning process* that can provide an opportunity for all participants to understand more clearly what they want to achieve together.
2. Second, it is a *discovery process* because it can expose hidden opportunities for growth (as well as threats to that growth), and it can reveal potential solutions for organizational problems that are of strategic importance.
3. Third, strategy formulation is a *decision process* that analyzes data, evaluates assumptions, prioritizes values and problems, and allocates resources and capabilities to adopt a realistic view of what the organization can and cannot undertake in the future.
4. Finally, strategic planning is an *innovation process* that requires openness to different views of how the organization can become more flexible and adaptable.

There are several incorrect assumptions about planning, and in the following sections we present three that seem to be the most problematic and compelling for keeping an organization vision-focused and strategy-directed.

Incorrect Assumption #1: Visioning and Planning Are Top-Down Activities

Traditionally, strategic planning has been undertaken as a leadership task and function. In this approach, the top management of an organization, sometimes with middle-level managers' input, meets to evaluate where the organization has been and to decide where it is going. One notable feature of organizational planning is that it is not a unitary science. That is, planning requires conceptual, technical, and interpersonal considerations, of which some senior managers may not be particularly knowledgeable or skilled. Thus, it is important to recognize that participants throughout the organization can be helpful in providing information and skill sets that complement those of the upper-level managers.

Although some managers are biased toward people on their team who are like them, it is the mark of confident leaders to gather around them people who have strengths and gifts they do not have. Once upon a time, Sheri worked for an organization that administered the Myers-Briggs Type Indicator (MBTI) to current employees with the goal of assessing how diverse personality types could lead to better collaborative working relationships. An added benefit was that it would also help determine gaps in departments so that the team members could discuss their work styles and how they might improve their results, ultimately ensuring the success of the organization. The process also allowed individual insight into work preferences and issues that were likely to interfere with productivity and enjoyment.

Surprisingly, Sheri's profile was the opposite of the human resource vice-president's profile, but that was one of the factors that the VP of HR considered as she selected her team. She sought to build a team that would not only complement her strengths, but also compensate for areas in which she needed improvement. Ultimately, she recognized that having someone with a different way of approaching problems, developing solutions, and making decisions was an advantage for her department, as well as for the health and success of the organization.

Some of the problems with viewing planning as a top-down activity also have to do with the political aspects of the organizational system. It is a function that involves political questions of power, accountability, and resource allocation; it is not value-free. Strategic planning involves decisions and trade-offs between different options, which may create the perception of unequal allocation of resources or opportunities to one or more of the organization's units or members. Therefore, when strategic planning is undertaken solely by the top and imposed on levels below, it has the potential to create division among employees—the very people who are required to implement it.

So, although it is necessarily true that top managers are presumed to have a "bird's eye view" of the organization and, therefore, planning should begin there, it is insufficient to depend on them for all strategic planning activities. For one thing, often the small details and tacit knowledge reside lower in the organization that make the formulation of strategic plans problematic. Without that information, the construction of a plan does not take into consideration as fully as it might the complexities between departments, processes, and systems throughout the organization. We are sure you have experienced plans that leave employees scratching their heads and wondering, "How could management have missed such an obvious thing?" What is often clear to employees is not always obvious to their managers.

So, managers that see strategic planning as primarily a top-down activity lose valuable gifts and talents possessed by members throughout the organization, create division among those members, and miss details that can be make or break the effectiveness of the strategy. It is no wonder that this assumption is often a main reason why strategic planning fails or has been abandoned in many organizations.

Incorrect Assumption #2: A Well-Conceived Strategy Gives You a Competitive Advantage

Another basic problem with strategy formulation and strategy execution has to do with *how* the strategy is conceived and executed. Although spending time on the planning and conceptualization phase is necessary, it is not sufficient to ensure success. Organizations must also spend time and resources on making sure that all the players understand the purpose for the strategy so that they implement it effectively.

Table 3.1 shows a sample of possible combinations of strategy conception and implementation so that we can delve a bit more deeply into potential barriers to success.

Table 3.1. Relationships between Strategy Conception and Implementation

		Strategy Implementation	
		Poorly implemented	**Well implemented**
Strategy Conception	*Poorly conceived*	**Fire!** Plan is reactionary, unrealistic, and arrogant. Short-lived and ineffective. Creates division and cynicism among employees. Almost always misses the mark and dies fairly quickly.	**Ready, fire!** Plan is typical of "fads" in which an organization spends resources on implementing a program/process that has been successful elsewhere, but that does not fit its context. Usually dies a slow death and is abandoned in time.
	Well conceived	**Ready, aim!** Plan is realistic and attainable, and involves multiple perspectives. It then sits on the shelf because no one understands how to make it work or understands his or her part in making it work; it is often implemented too late. Short-lived, if implemented at all.	**Ready, aim, fire!** Plan takes into account many perspectives and the specific organizational context. Continual monitoring of effectiveness and adjustment of plan. Involves and engages all participants. Has the best potential for success over the long term.

Poorly Conceived and Poorly Implemented Plans

This is the "train wreck" quadrant. Not only do the plans miss the mark in terms of realistic possibilities and market understanding, their implementation (if it happens at all) is generally scattered and almost never accomplishes much of anything, except to create cynics and skeptics about what direction the organization is going in and whether it is likely to actually get there. One example of this is the manner in which some organizations approach restructuring or downsizing.

Asked by the board of directors to reduce head count, the new president of a consumer product organization did not really understand the way the staff was organized. Instead of asking and getting input from those who knew the business, he noticed that members of the telemarketing department worked out of their homes. He had not ever met or talked with the telemarketers, but he thought laying them off would be an easy way to remove "heads" from the organization chart. Without first consulting with the manager of the telemarketing staff, he instructed her to eliminate that division. The manager told the president that the staff was paid on 100 percent commission, so eliminating them would not save any money to the bottom line. In fact, she reasoned that it would actually hurt sales because the team members had developed relationships with their customers and generated a substantial amount of revenue for the organization. The president explained that it *would* make a difference, because his instructions were to reduce head count, not spending, and ordered her to proceed with the terminations, which she did.

The company paid to have all the telemarketers' equipment sent back to the office and sent a note to their customers telling them the news. All the customers were livid and followed the telemarketers to their next positions . . . with the competition! That year, the company's sales were the worst in its 70-year history. The following year the president decided to call the telemarketers back to their former positions. However, they were all gainfully employed by then and chose to stay where they were. The company had to start from scratch, hiring, training, and sending out computer equipment to the new staff so they could work at home. Moreover, they also had to find new customers. This example highlights the "Fire!" mentality of a plan that had little thought put into it, was not discussed with the key players, and was poorly executed as well.

Poorly Conceived but Well-Implemented Plans

At some point in your professional lives many of you have experienced the "fad of the month" in which top managers run into buddies on the golf course or in a meeting and learn that they have adopted the latest and greatest approach to running organizations, managing supply chains, or marketing products and services. You know the ones we mean: TQM, Six Sigma, Theory Z, self-managed teams, JIT, and FISH! Philosophy, and there are many more. A new management fad means endless meetings, new buzzwords, and extra work that drives you crazy or puts your company even further behind its competition.

A fad, by nature, has simple precepts. In fact, that is why a fad is so poorly conceived. Fads reduce complex ideas, tasks, or situations to a small number of factors, dimensions, or characteristics. However, they are often implemented well, because they make few cognitive demands on people, take relatively little time to absorb and master, and are easily communicated. As with most things in life, if it looks too good to be true, it probably is.

To be fair, it is not that the concepts and techniques of some of these approaches fail. Rather, it is that fads imply a quick and easy solution to extremely complex problems. They propose a general approach that is presumed to be relevant to a universe of organizations—a "one size fits all" mentality.

One study demonstrated how many of the popular management fads in the past 30 years have resulted in lower than expected results, poor returns on investment, and unwanted consequences.[3] The common thread of failure was not making the necessary changes to ensure that the technique worked, given the people, technology, and operations in the particular organizational context.

Interestingly, fads are usually conceived alongside the current business problems they are proposed to solve. For example, many of the popular quality management approaches of the 1980s and 1990s occurred as the United States was losing market share to Japan because of poor quality. Organizations adopted Japanese approaches for all sorts of manufacturing and service operations, most with short-lived results.

Another notable feature of fads is that they are not particularly radical in their approach. Most of the time they are merely restating well-established beliefs that managers have held over time; they just usually do it with new vocabulary. For example, "Just-in-Time approach" is nothing more than the belief that organizations spend a lot of money carrying inventory that is not needed right away; "Kaizen" just means that if all organizational members are aware of problems and focus on continually improving how something is done, waste will be eliminated, and the processes will be more effective and efficient. See? Nothing in these fads is rocket science, and nothing is really new.

By far, though, the worst part of fads is their psychological effect on employees. Attempting fads and then watching them die (slowly or quickly) makes it that much harder to engage employees in effective solutions to real problems, especially if their leaders have a history of hopping from one fad to another. Although managers usually have the best intentions when they adopt a fad, and they follow the prescription of the fad in its implementation, when they do not consider the situation in their own organizations, the strategy eventually fades into the sunset.

Well-Conceived but Poorly Implemented Plans

Picture an organization with a solid, clear mission that has been doing well for decades; then the marketplace changes. What should the company do? Most of you are probably saying, "Change, of course!" One problem with market reactive change is that it is usually too slow, primarily because the organization is trying to adapt to changes that have already happened in the environment.

Unfortunately, many organizations are slow off the starting block because they spend an inordinate amount of time on the conceptualization of what they should do, but then don't take the same care in making sure the change is executed effectively. Consider the following as a classic example.

For decades, Junkfood Joe's (not its real name) sold premium products that contained high fat and caloric content, but were very tasty. The organization was successful in its market and had good brand recognition of its name and products. Following the introduction of the Food and Drug Administration's (FDA's) revised dietary requirements in 2002, the United States began to see more emphasis placed on healthy and organically grown food, rather than on processed food. In 2007, a new president for Junkfood Joe's was hired.

The management team had been contemplating changing its focus for years and suggested to the new president the idea that the company should offer a low-fat option or a healthy counterpart. However, the president was leery of how radical that might be perceived, particularly given the company's market niche. He didn't want the company to fail on "his watch." So, instead of introducing new, healthier food options, the president chose to decrease the size of the company's staple products while increasing the price, hoping consumers wouldn't notice, thereby making a greater profit for the company and, of course, making him look like a hero.

The team went on a three-day retreat to a nearby resort and crafted an outline of what a new vision statement might look like, identified several new goals for the next two to three years, and began developing the strategies that they would adopt. They also spent about $10,000 of the company's money at the resort!

Part of the plan called for the organization to change the look of the logo. The president's best friend's wife worked at a marketing design firm, so he hired her to change the logo, and then spent another couple of months haggling over which design the company should pick. Meanwhile, Junkfood Joe's closest competitor (and several others, as well) introduced new, healthier products at prices similar to the current not-so-healthy premium priced ones. As a result, Junkfood Joe's had a new sleek logo, redesigned all their promotional material and packaging, and then proceeded to have the worst sales year in its history. What started off as a well-intentioned and well-conceived idea ended up badly because the implementation had serious flaws and major delays. The organization ultimately kept the new logo and color scheme, but it had to sell its leftover inventory at a huge discount to try to recoup some of its investment. Had the president listened to the management team, the company could have introduced a new line of healthier products and competed successfully instead of getting trampled by the competition.

Organizations that develop strategies that are reactionary are not usually as successful as those that are proactive. The environment changes much too quickly. It is rather like rafting on white water—by the time you realize you are in the midst of it, all you can do is paddle furiously to stay afloat.

Well-Conceived and Well-Implemented Plans

Finding the balance between strategy conceptualization and its execution is an art and a science. Many organizations that do strategic planning adopt a more *prescriptive* approach; that is, they begin with the "where-we-are-now" mentality and then develop new strategies for the future. This is a linear and rational approach that defines the objectives in advance and puts the main elements in place before the implementation commences. Critics of this approach have argued that an *emergent* approach is more realistic and adaptable to ongoing changes.[4] In this view, the specific actions an organization takes continue to develop as the strategy proceeds, thereby allowing it to evolve incrementally and continuously. In essence, the emergent strategy is centered on understanding the environment in which the organization operates.

However, an emergent approach can be frightening to top managers. How will they maintain control? How can the organization possibly be that flexible? On the other hand, the problem with prescriptive strategy is that it presumes that human beings can anticipate what will happen in the future—not a likely bet, as we have seen recently with financial crises, hurricanes, and elections! Let's consider one example that demonstrates how both a prescriptive and an emergent approach might work.

A well-known consumer products company sells products of which the majority is bought between October and January. The company needs almost 12,000 employees during that time, but only needs about 20 percent of them the rest of the year. In a typical prescriptive scenario, the senior management team would decide the target number of products to sell or the revenue target for the year. The top managers would then inform the HR staff of the sales and revenue targets and have human resources find the sales and production people to make it happen. The HR staff then engages in a massive "manhunt" for temporary employees for October-January employment, likely using every recruiting resource they can imagine. They manage to find most of the new staff by August, get the paperwork completed, and inform the new temporary employees of their start dates.

However, imagine that at the end of August there is a major disruption in the supply chain because of a weather-related occurrence. The company, having only dealt with one major supplier, cannot get a fundamental ingredient for its products. The new employees are told not to show up for work, as there is no work to do until the ingredient can be sourced from another supplier. As a result, by the time the ingredient actually arrives, only 5,000 employees are still available, the rest having taken another job in the meantime. Disaster in the making!

Now consider an emergent approach in which the company's top management team meets with representatives from all stakeholders, including human resources, the suppliers, sales, production, and finance. They discuss the environment in which they operate, focusing on the current and potential problems and opportunities in that environment. They then acknowledge where in the company they may have vulnerability and how they can minimize it. In this case, the team recognizes that a major vulnerability is having only one supplier, as well as the staffing challenge of finding a large number of temporary workers. Their planning, then, focuses on how to minimize these vulnerabilities. In this case, they decide to develop multiple scenarios for how to do that. Each participant understands his or her role in the plan, and the team members meet each month to review their progress, as well as to reevaluate the likelihood of each scenario. Interestingly, as alternative scenarios are being developed, an HR staff member finds a group of retired people called "Workampers" who live in campers and travel from seasonal job to seasonal job year round.[5] They are a reliable group of people and perfectly adapted to the strategy that emerges. As the August disruption occurs, the team is able to quickly put in place an alternative plan to minimize the damage to production and sales, adjusting as the environment changes.

Clearly, strategy formulation and implementation are not independent activities, but interdependent ones that require involvement and engagement by all stakeholders to ensure effectiveness and sustainability. Assuming a top-down approach to strategy often results in organizations that "Ready" themselves without the ammunition to implement the strategy, "Aim" with no clear target, and "Fire!" before they are ready.

Incorrect Assumption #3: A Clear Vision Engages Employees

Though it is likely true that "where there is no vision, the people perish," the assumption that a clear vision will engage employees is, again, a necessary but insufficient condition. Many organizations spend a lot of time and resources coming up with the perfect picture of what their future should look like, only to fail to measure all of their strategies, plans, and operations by how they are helping the organization achieve that future. If a vision is supposed to give direction to an organization and its members, there must be an indication of how to achieve it. In other words, a vision can only get employees engaged if they believe it can be done and know how to make it come true.

Think of Olympic athletes. Presumably they have a vision of winning a medal (probably their vision is the gold). But just having that vision does not necessarily tell them what they need to do to achieve it. That only comes from the understanding of what it really takes to win an Olympic medal—things like natural athleticism, a lot of practice, mental toughness, and financial resources, among others. Organizations are similar. They may have painted a vision to become the best in their industry at customer service, but just saying so doesn't make it so. The vision may make their employees *want* to be the best at customer service, but if they don't know what it takes to do that, their enthusiasm and engagement will wane.

Imagine for a moment something you would like to become. Maybe a scratch golfer, a platinum recording artist, or the CEO of a *Fortune* 100 firm? Whatever it is, you must take a multitude of steps, starting from where you are now, that lead to where your vision becomes a reality. How do you maintain your direction toward that vision? What is necessary to even get started? What will keep you motivated to continue working toward it? That is the challenge for you, and that is the challenge for all organizations that want to move from where they are to what they wish to become.

So, besides a clear vision, what is really required to get employees focused and engaged? We suggest that the missing pieces are clear expectations for behavior and continuous involvement in evaluating their progress toward the vision. As we have stated throughout this chapter, if one of the major business problems is keeping an organization vision-focused and strategy-directed, all members have to be engaged on a continual basis. That means they must feel a positive emotional attachment to the vision. Such a feeling will create a connection, resulting in their willingness and an ability to keep focused and engaged. Including employees as an integral part of creating the vision, involving them in solving problems, and removing barriers to the achievement of the vision will allow better alignment with the organizational strategy. As a result, they will understand clearly what they are doing and why they are doing it, ultimately allowing for a competitive advantage. This leads us to one of the primary barriers to effective strategy implementation: translation of ideas into employee action.

Translating Vision and Strategy into Action

There are several prerequisites for translating vision and strategy into action. The first of these is *realism*. It's a nice aspiration for the smallest player in a market to set a goal of being number one—but is it realistic? Remember we want to motivate employees for an extended period of time. Being aspirational and challenging is great, but you end up doing more harm than good if you articulate an unachievable vision. Visions that are perceived to be unreachable and strategies that appear unrealistic cause employees to give up more easily, and, even more harmful, the staff internalizes the failure to achieve them.

Television is a great example of how stations adjust their strategies to be realistic within their environments. For example, during "sweeps week," most television stations realize they are not going to be able to compete head-to-head with the season finales of the most popular shows, so they air reruns. During the

Super Bowl time slot, competing stations make conscious decisions not to compete with the most highly watched sporting event of the year.

Businesses, likewise, make similar decisions when it comes to crafting realistic visions, achievable goals, and doable strategies. Consider small, family-owned businesses. They do not try to compete with the "big box stores" on price or volume; instead, these organizations motivate their employees to provide high-quality service, knowing that they can surpass the competition by focusing on a service strategy. Not only will their service orientation keep their current customers, but word-of-mouth will likely earn them even more new customers.

The second prerequisite is *specificity*. Who could disagree with a vision that says, "Deliver excellence in customer service"? But statements like these are so generic as to be useless. How will the organization differentiate itself? What is the specific time frame allotted to working toward the vision? How will value be created by sticking to the plan? At the end of the day, both leaders and employees should be able to articulate clearly the answers to these and other relevant questions.

The third requirement is to *measure what matters*. Peter Drucker's statement that "what gets measured, gets managed" is true. The key is to determine just what matters in our organizations, and this will vary depending on the organization.

Several years ago, Dale and a colleague published a study on the key performance indicators in call centers.[6] The strategy for many call centers is centered on speed: Answer the call quickly, deal with the problem quickly, get the customer off the phone quickly. These measures were kept daily, and the call center operators were trained, evaluated, and rewarded on minimizing the time spent on calls. However, from a customer's point of view, speed was not the most important evaluation criterion—solving the problem and the quality of that solution were their main concern. So, despite the detailed measures and attention paid to "amount of time to answer phone," "amount of time on call," and "amount of time customer spent waiting for answer," what really mattered (and what ultimately needed to be managed and rewarded) ended up being "percentage of problems solved the first time."

The importance of having a discussion across the organization about the things that really matter cannot be understated. Again, this cannot be just a top management decision, primarily because of the reasons we discussed earlier about the tacit and explicit knowledge of front-line employees. Asking customers, employees, suppliers, and other stakeholders what matters to them may be surprising to top managers who are often most concerned with the financial aspects of the business to the frequent exclusion of the customer or employee experience. For example, consider the differences between bankers and their customers in what matters to each.

The Gallup organization's November 2012 Gallup Daily Tracking poll concerning confidence in banking found that the percentage of Americans who had "a great deal" or "quite a lot" of confidence in the U.S. banking system fell to a record low of 15 percent from the previous 22 percent in 2008. At the same time, the percentage of Americans who had "very little" or "no" confidence in the U.S. banking system reached a record high of 42 percent.[7] Dennis Jacobe, chief economist for Gallop, offered the explanation that bankers often see things strictly from a financial perspective, whereas customers become emotionally engaged in their banking experiences. He put it this way:

> Bankers are also doing things like overtly passing on costs in the form of fees, which infuriates the customers who are expected to pay them. And bankers are also making cuts in customer service, which not only angers customers, but it basically encourages them to walk out the door. Some banks have reacted by cutting back on employees. That may make financial sense in the short term. The fewer

people on the payroll, the lower the operating costs, and cost cutting is required when revenues are declining.

But . . . customer-facing employees remain consumers' most preferred provider of banking services and may be a bank's best hope for promoting customer engagement. . . . The most powerful drivers of customer loyalty and engagement remain branch visits and call center interactions with a real person. So the last place to cut should be front-line employees, because when fewer people are providing what matters most to customers, loyalty and engagement can easily take a significant hit. . . . Customers become engaged only when emotional needs are met: they feel pride and passion for the brand they bank with, they believe the bank has integrity, and they're confident they'll always be treated well and fairly. It's financially imperative that banks provoke this response. Fully engaged retail banking customers are *much* more likely to say they intend to open a new account or take out a new loan over the next three months than are actively disengaged customers. And actively disengaged customers are much more likely to switch banks.

What is true for customers seems also true for employees: When employees are emotionally connected to what the organization is doing, believe that their managers have integrity, and are confident they will be treated fairly, it is not difficult to keep them vision-focused and strategy-directed. In the next section we provide one example of how you, in your own organization, can help make this happen, laying the foundation to help resolve one of top managers' most common business problems.

Sample Solution #1: Determining Core Values as an Organization

As we mentioned earlier, dispelling the myth that visioning is a top-down activity is the first step in your process, and creating a well-conceived and well-implemented strategy is crucial for keeping people focused on the road to achieving that vision. But how does one do all this? We'd like to lay out an example process you can use to make sure everyone is on the same path. Our suggested sample process has four advantages:

1. It engages the hearts and minds of employees and managers in the common welfare of all organizational stakeholders.
2. It creates opportunities for new ideas and strategies to emerge that would not have ordinarily come to light with the involvement of only top managers.
3. It highlights the areas in which employees will have the most angst, concern, and resistance.
4. It ensures buy-in and agreement with the vision (not just compliance), as well as the strategies necessary to achieve it.

Step #1: Small Group Gatherings to Determine Core Values

The first step is to have your senior manager (for example, president, CEO, executive director) announce that he or she would like to have the organization create new core values and a new vision. At first, the employees will probably not believe that he or she really means to authentically involve them. This is primarily because it may never have happened before or, if such a thing has been attempted in the past, it probably failed miserably and, therefore, the employees do not trust that the same thing won't happen again. But this is part and parcel of any employee involvement activity, so take a deep breath and start anyway.

The most successful way to begin this part of the process is to have a series of gatherings with interested employees. Do not worry if the turnout is small in the beginning. As the process starts taking shape and people see that management is actually listening and using their ideas, more people will get involved. It is best to limit these gatherings to no more than 30 people at each one. At these gatherings, serve some type of food (it doesn't matter what) and nonalcoholic beverages. Even a "brown bag lunch" invitation where everyone brings a lunch can work. The point is that eating together is important to the community-building process, and determining an organization's core values definitely requires a sense of community!

"Core values" are those values that form the foundation by which we conduct ourselves, and they are a constant, even when the environment around an organization changes. Core values are not descriptions of the work we do; rather, they underlie our work, and they describe how we interact with each other to fulfill our mission. They are the behavioral guidelines we use every day. Therefore, rather than impose behavioral guidelines on employees (which many organizations routinely do), we prefer to let employees articulate their own. It is far more productive in the long run, and, as we mentioned previously, it creates engagement and acceptance, not just compliance with rules and policies.

The following step-by-step process is a means of getting to the values that are deeply held by your organization's members.[8] Start by reading the following scenario to the whole group:

Imagine you are moving from a large home to a much smaller one. Therefore, as you carefully pack all your belongings, there are some things you are sure you will need, other things you think you might need, and still other things you cannot bear to leave behind. As you pack, you are not certain which is which. Organizational change is like this. You know you must change, but you do not know exactly how or where you will ultimately find yourselves. The baggage you load for the move includes many values. Some values are of greater importance, others of lesser importance. Some are clearly shared by everyone in the group. Others are not. Some values are so important to an individual, that, unless everyone shares that value, that individual cannot be part of the group. Others are so important to an individual, that, unless that individual has the freedom to cherish that value in the group, the individual cannot be part of the group. Only the move itself can test which values are most important to all.

Now, create smaller groups and assign a facilitator (someone from human resources would be ideal for this). It is optimal to have seven to eight members in each of the smaller groups. Give the following instructions to each smaller group (see text box).

The facilitator should then invite each small group to share its chosen top three values. Are there common trends? Are there surprises?

Step #2: Organization-Wide Responses

Every organization experiences times of stress during transitions or crises. With a few managers and employees, describe one stressful time in the life of the organization during the past 10 years. This stressful time could have been joyous or tragic, and it might have resulted in good feelings or bad feelings. In times of stress, people behave in certain natural or habitual ways, and these behavior patterns reveal what they truly value. Here are some questions to help you:

- What caused the stress?
- How did people react to the stress?
- What resulted from the stressful time?
- What core values were revealed by the behavior of the organization's managers and employees during this stressful time?

Step #1: Your small group of people will share this new house, and none of you can take everything with you. *Make as comprehensive a list as possible of all the values each person holds in your small group.* This is your inventory of all the values you hold. Some values may be precious to a few; others are precious to many. Some values may be more important to some and not to others. List them all. Don't try to prioritize them. Let's just get the big picture.

Step #2: Now imagine that you are loading the moving van. Remember: Your group must share the house. You cannot take everything with you. *Together, choose the top 10 values that you want to move to your new home.* Set the others aside for the moment. We'll see how full the moving van is afterward, and if we can load a few more values on, we will! Sometimes values in our inventory look so much alike that we can put them together creatively. Be sure, however, that they are still clearly understood. If so, load them!

Step #3: Good news! Even after loading the top 10 values onto the moving van, we still have some room. *Choose two more values that are precious to the entire group and add those.* Now you have 12.

Step #4: Now imagine your moving van gets stuck going up a steep hill. You need to lighten the load. From the top 12 values loaded *select the seven most important values you will keep to carry forward.* Yes, it is permissible to combine two values into a larger value that includes the essence of both, but make sure the larger value is still clearly understandable by everyone in the group! Core values that become too vague will be like stale food that has lost its nutritional value: You can carry it a long way, but it will do you no good to eat it.

Step #5: You made it up the hill, but it has been a long day of moving. You are weary but determined to press forward to your destination. Slowly, your small group has bonded together, but it has not always been easy. Negotiation has sometimes been heated, and compromise has sometimes been painful. And yet here is one last unexpected obstacle! While crossing a street about a mile from your new home, a huge fissure has opened before you. There is only one thing to do. You must abandon the moving van! Unfortunately, members of the group may carry only what they can manage on their backs! *From the top seven absolutely most important values left in the van, choose the three values that your group simply cannot live without.* You may not combine or add values. You must prioritize three from the seven.

Step #6: Knowing what you know now, *from among the top three values from all groups, rank in order of importance the top 10 values you cherish above all.*

Now pose the following questions in an organization-wide survey, or ask people to respond via e-mail (or, in the case where anonymity is crucial, by letter):

In times of stress, this organization seems to naturally do certain things, and these natural reactions seem to reveal certain values.

This is what we always do:

_____

These are the real values such habits reveal:

_____

Now compare these behavior patterns, and the values they reveal, to the "top 10" lists that emerged from the small group gatherings.

Are there positive values that should be added to the "top 10" lists?

Are there negative realities that contradict the values in the "top 10" lists?

The purpose of this information is that organizations often sanitize their core values. In other words, when top managers "create" core values, they are usually aspirational values, *not* ones that describe how the organization actually behaves or is truly seen by others. Step 2 in this process allows feedback about what values presently guide the organization's actions.

The final piece of this process is for top management to decide on five core values and have the organization as a whole adopt them as its own. Once the entire staff sees that there is consensus on "who we really are," the vision and strategies for attaining the vision can be crafted.

Once the core values are adopted, creating a shared vision can proceed using the same process. By this time, a majority of employees will be engaged in the process, so it is crucial not to abandon their interest or focus by having top management create the vision and then impose it on the employees. Visioning is a creative process, whereas strategy development is a more concrete process. Using employees' creativity will keep them motivated and interested in your business because it engages both their hearts and their minds. The strategies necessary to pursue the vision will most likely be done by managers; however, we caution that getting relevant employee input will only help strengthen trust and commitment.

Common Business Problem #2: Playing to Win or Playing Not to Lose: How Do We Become More Competitive in Our Marketplace?

"Competition has been shown to be useful up to a certain point and no further, but cooperation, which is the thing we must strive for today, begins where competition leaves off."

—*Franklin D. Roosevelt*

Respondents to our survey were worried about how they could remain or become competitive in a marketplace that seems to change on a dime. It seemed to us as we read various responses that the underlying issues were uncertainty and the fear it engendered among all the organization's stakeholders. One respondent captured this idea well:

> Uncertainty fosters distrust, which makes recruiting top talent harder, retaining talent harder, motivating people harder, and getting management to make decisions in a timely fashion harder. People are nervous . . . under all of that is the feeling of a lack of security and fear that must be overcome.

Before we begin discussing some of the ways to understand and manage market competitiveness, it is probably wise to spend a few minutes looking at the basic nature of competition.

What Do We Mean by Competition?

Competition arises whenever at least two parties try to obtain an outcome or outcomes that cannot be shared. As shared inhabitants of planet Earth, we compete naturally for resources (for example water, food) of which there is a finite supply. Thus, whatever water or food person A or animal B consumes, person C or animal D cannot consume. In this way, we could say that natural resources are perceived to be a fixed pie.[1] The mythical "fixed pie" mindset leads us to interpret competitive situations as purely win-lose propositions; that is, whatever you get, I don't get. We see this happening both between and within organizations.

Competition *between* business organizations most often occurs when at least one other firm provides products or services to the same group of customers, patients, or clients. Competition *within* business organizations can be seen among employees, among units or departments, and among values and goals throughout the organization. Both types (between and within) can occur in three different ways, all of which present different challenges for an organization.

Direct competition usually involves products or services that are essentially the same. Between organizations this means that each organization produces or provides something that is exactly substitutable by another organization: Kleenex versus Puffs, Geico auto insurance versus Progressive auto insurance, University of X versus University of Y. Each provides a product or service that is generally perceived by customers as essentially the same. Therefore, gaining a customer means providing something beyond that which a direct competitor provides.

Within organizations direct competition focuses more on the skills and competencies of employees or the services provided by departments/subunits. For example, many of you may have several choices in your organization for who might provide help and support for your computer database (for example, an IT department member or your co-worker who is a whiz at databases). Each source can provide exactly the help you need, and, therefore, each is in direct competition for your "business." In this instance, gaining a competitive advantage within an organization means providing the service or help in the most efficient and effective way, paying particular attention to redundancies between and among subunits and employees.

Indirect competition is a bit more complex and involves products, services, or experiences that are different, but substitutable: a car versus a minivan, margarine versus butter, hospital emergency room versus urgent care clinic, large university versus small college. Inside an organization, indirect competition might occur because of competing goals or values among various departments. Here is a classic example: A sales department has the goal to increase the number of unique products sold, whereas a production department has the goal to decrease the cost (or increase the efficiency) of production. However, producing more unique products requires greater production time and, therefore, costs more. Therefore, in this situation, the goals of sales and production departments are indirectly competitive—achieving the one means foregoing, or at least reducing, the other.

Finally, resource competition occurs when organizations compete for scarce resources, such as money, materials, labor, or time. Customers, for example, have only so much money to spend; there are only so many qualified workers in the labor market; there is only so much lumber available in Tokyo. Inside organizations only so much time and money are available (that is, departments and projects compete for budget dollars) to do what a particular unit wants or needs to do. Therefore, the choice or decision to expend resources in a firm is a competitive one. Several of the respondents to our survey actually seemed to be focused more on this third type of competition, as several stated their frustrations in these ways:

- How can we charge our customers enough to cover the investment in new technologies to remain competitive?
- How do we compete globally with limited infrastructure?
- How do we find good people with the skills we need when we can't pay high salaries?

Note that these respondents are basically stating what they perceive to be the problem, the cause, *and* the solution in their questions. For example, "How do we charge our customers enough?" is stated as the perceived problem to investing in new technologies, which is then assumed to be the cause of not remaining competitive; thus, the natural conclusion to this train of thought is that if we could charge our customers enough, we would remain competitive. Likewise, "finding good people with the skills we need" (the problem) is assumed to be caused by not paying high enough salaries; therefore, if we could pay high salaries, we would find good people with the skills we need.

We don't know what, if any, objective data these respondents have to support these assertions, but it is quite possible that they have potentially misprocessed or ignored the true drivers of what their organizations really require to remain competitive. At the very least, it is likely that they see only one "solution" to the stated "problem." One dangerous approach to solving any problem is to state it in terms of a solution. We will return to this concern in a moment.

The Benefits and Challenges of Market Competitiveness

By now, you can see that there are multiple ways to look at business competition, and there are multiple benefits and challenges to each of them. Social Darwinists claim that competition serves as a mechanism for determining the best-suited group to operate in any given environment—economically, politically, legally, ecologically.[2] The bottom line in competition is that outcomes occur that are both good and not-so-good for multiple stakeholders when an organization is engaged in market competition.

Competition among businesses can be beneficial in that it can result in better outcomes for consumers, but it can also be detrimental when it drains valuable resources and energy from the firm. For employees, competition can cause psychological and physical stress, long work hours, abusive working relationships, and poor working conditions, despite the fact that such competition may result in financial gain for the owners and shareholders and, thereby, provide continuing employment and salaries for employees.

Value and goal competition within organizations can be confusing for all members and generally takes an organization and its employees off in disparate directions, only to result in unfocused mission, vision, and strategy. As a result, decision-making seems capricious, jobs and tasks appear disconnected from each other, and performance and morale decline.

The key is to understand *why* an organization is having difficulty becoming or remaining competitive. We now turn our attention to two sources of what we believe form the basis for the "market competiveness" problems that concern our respondents. We also examine a few of the drivers and indicators that can help organizations learn to become more competitive.

Source #1: Not Adopting a Learning Orientation

Basically, to achieve a competitive advantage in their markets, organizations must identify and satisfy customer needs more effectively than their competitors do. The next logical question then becomes, how does a firm do this? One prerequisite to maintaining a long-term competitive advantage is to improve the processing of critical market information. To discover what customers want and need and to provide it faster than their competitors are the main sources of competitive advantage, particularly in markets that change constantly.

Earlier we noted that successful organizations (that is, profitable organizations) do not always pay attention to critical information, or their managers perceive incorrectly that they are handling any issues that may affect the organization's success or failure. These are crucial problems because they ultimately lead to a primary market fit problem: uncertainty.

"Uncertainty" means that there is a lack of reliable and valid information. If an organization is not collecting critical market information along the supply chain—in other words, things like information concerning vendors of raw or finished goods, availability of service providers, design of products, prices of capital equipment, speed of transport, availability of warehousing or labor, and customer preferences—it is highly likely that they will miss signals of changes in their market, particularly when markets change quickly.

For example, one local retailer was interested in surveying its customers to learn more about their spending habits and preferences for gift-giving. They had hundreds of kiosks throughout the nation, and these could easily serve as a collection point for their customers' e-mail addresses or phone numbers so that they could survey them later. The bad news was that the retailer didn't realize the missed opportunity until midway through its busiest season. The good news was that it was able to move quickly enough even then to add contact information as a last step while the customers were checking out. Although some customers were unwilling to share their personal information, the retailer decided to offer a 20 percent discount on their next purchase if they would provide an e-mail address or phone number. As a result, the percentage of e-mails and phone numbers collected began to soar.

Combatting uncertainty requires an organization to adopt a learning orientation. The rate at which an organization learns to successfully and quickly process critical information so it can satisfy customers' expressed and latent needs is what provides the primary market advantage. A learning orientation challenges the assumptions that frame the organization's relationship with its environment. To put it another way, it requires us to question everything that we have previously accepted as fact and to look at it with new eyes. As Sean Covey recounted, "Instead of playing to win, I was playing not to lose. It reminds me of the story I once heard about two friends being chased by a bear, when one turned to the other and said, 'I just realized that I don't need to outrun the bear; I only need to outrun you.'"[3] Seeing more clearly the underlying assumptions we make about our markets, our competitors, and our own internal competitive issues will help us learn how to reframe our problems and rethink the solutions to them.

Returning to the example about the market competitiveness frustrations voiced by some of our respondents, recall we said that stating the problem in terms of the solution was dangerous. Here are some reasons why.

First, it narrows the learning field to consider only the solution stated. If I think that the problem with finding good people with the skills I need is due to my ability to pay them, then I will not be looking at any other solution *except* figuring out how to raise salaries. Second, it narrows the learning field to only those people who have expertise or information about that one solution. If I think that increasing salary is the solution, then I'll be seeking advice and implementing recommendations from only those people who have something to do with compensation, either in my organization or from an outside consultant. As a result, I will miss out on several potential solutions that may not involve salary, and I will probably not ask for help from other people unless they have expertise or decision-making capability in compensation.

Learning within the organization occurs through processes that create new knowledge, as well as how to use and transform existing knowledge. Specifically, when an organization seems to be doing well, it takes an open-minded management team to begin to question what the "next big thing" is and then to use that knowledge to position the organization to take advantage of it. Failing to adopt a learning orientation leaves the organization vulnerable to its competitors and to the whims of its customers. From an organization-environment fit perspective, a learning orientation raises questions and challenges assumptions about how well an organization will fit its market in the future—even when it seems to be doing quite well at the moment!

The Role of *Unlearning*

Before we can begin to learn new information about how competitive we are in our market, as well as what to do next, *unlearning* is usually required. For firms to unlearn obsolete market knowledge and norms, they must get rid of the perceptual filters that bias which new information is attended to and acted on. Some of this unlearning may involve questioning rules, policies, processes, behavioral norms, and other internal ways business is conducted, as well as the external market information. This step will help the organization with both continuous improvements and breakthrough innovations. Organizations with a commitment to learning encourage, and some even require, employees to question the information and norms that guide their behavior.

But how do you secure a commitment to learning from managers and employees?

As we discussed in Chapter 3, it begins with having a shared vision across the organization. First and foremost, without a common vision, individuals are less likely to share information with each other, because they may be operating with a "fixed pie" mindset. Second, if we don't agree on the assumptions about our market and how we conduct business, we will probably also not agree on the interpretation of market information and, thus, we cannot respond quickly to emerging trends or problems. And, just as importantly, the lack of a universally understood organizational vision also lowers the motivation of everybody to learn.

As we have already noted, core aspects of a vision are that it is universally known, understood, and used in a manner that gives the organization a sense of purpose and direction. If people from the top to the bottom of the organization understand what they are trying to accomplish, then it becomes much easier to see whether they are on-track or off-track along the way.

Besides having a shared vision, a commitment to learning also requires open-mindedness on the part of both management and employees. The ability to question long-held beliefs, assumptions, and routines is necessary to unlearn them and to free up our minds so that new approaches are sought. This is difficult for some managers, especially those who have a high need for control, but it is crucial. One's ego must take a back seat to the higher calling for accurate, reliable information. Once again, it is the problem of information misprocessing or denial of reality that poses the biggest barrier to establishing a learning orientation.

If we return for a moment to a couple of the specific concerns mentioned about market competitiveness, we can see that an attention to learning could be extremely beneficial in addressing these issues before they get out of hand:

- The quality of an organization's products or services is similar to competitors': Money must be spent to increase the quality of the products or services.
- Products or services have a small market share compared to competitors': There is a need for increased expenditure for marketing resources.

Notice that in both cases, the first part of each statement is, in actuality, a statement about what the organization perceives as the problem of "not being competitive." The second part of the statement is a "solution." However, what is missing is the driver or cause. In other words, by these statements alone, we don't know specifically how having similar quality to competitors or having a smaller market share create a competitiveness problem, and, moreover, why it is occurring. As we said before, jumping to the solution to spend more money on quality improvements or increasing one's marketing resources before the causes or drivers of problems are known can be dangerous.

What we need here are leading indicators that would allow an organization to learn critical information while there is still time to change what it is doing or how it is doing it. The next section discusses guidelines, in general, about identifying and establishing a few indicators that provide the best information to make decisions.

Leading Indicators for Market Fit

Deciding on the most appropriate leading indicators begins with asking the correct questions in the correct order for your organization. You may have noted that the five common business problems that form the basis for the chapter titles in this book are formulated as questions:

- How do we keep vision-focused and strategy-directed?
- How do we become more competitive?
- How do we deal with all the changing laws and regulations?
- How do we attract and retain the most competent talent? and
- How do we deal with a changing society?

The wording is intentional. The questions do not presume any perspective, nor do they suggest potential causes or solutions within them. This is important because it allows for multiple voices, wide-ranging causes, and creative solutions to bubble up in the process. Once these questions are asked and fully answered, finding indicators that provide critical information is much easier. Although there is no hard and fast rule about which indicators organizations should be measuring, there are a few guidelines:[4]

1. The indicators must enable you to forecast the principal revenue and cost drivers of your business, division, or function.
2. The indicators must be simple to understand, coherent, and actionable at multiple levels in the company.
3. The leading indicators must comprise a small, but balanced, set.

The first thing to remember is that the revenue and cost drivers will be different for every organization, although in most cases there are a few similar ones across organizations. For example, most organizations would consider changes in customer/client behavior to be a useful determination of potential revenue. You might remember in Chapter 3 we mentioned the problem of forecasting product inventory that the VP of retail faced. The change in customer behavior (waiting to buy products until after the price was marked down) was the primary driver of the company's revenue fluctuation.

Another driver might be "service quality," in which deficiencies in technicians' skills or the inattentiveness of sales representatives in returning customer phone calls are found to lead to fewer customer purchases in following months. Again, depending on your organization's sources of revenue, you will need to determine what is really driving the increase or decrease in the revenue side of the business. This requires extensive conversation with top managers and the managers of subunits within the organization, as well as a bit of detective work to gather objective, reliable data about those drivers of change.

Not all parts of a market act in the same way. That is to say that the customers who drive fluctuations in revenue may not be the same ones who produce most of the company's profit. To use a banking example, it is a fact that most loans and mortgages get paid on time, and these reliable customers produce most of a bank's profits. In reality, only a small subset of customers have poor credit and payment behavior. Although these marginal customers produce revenue for the bank in the good economic times as a result of the high fees and interest rates charged to them, they also require banks to have high reserves on hand to cover bad debt and loan defaults in the leaner economic times.

Similarly, the drivers of costs are also varied in most organizations. Perhaps there is a decreased capacity to produce goods because of equipment problems, supplier shortages, or an inability to find qualified workers. Costs of materials, inventories, energy, and labor have continued to increase for many organizations. Again, numerous potential drivers and indicators can alert you to changes that are coming. The key is in understanding those factors in your organization, as well as their affect, so that one can anticipate when and how much to shift resources or acquire additional resources to keep the organization competitive.

One specific example is a company that sold meat and cheese and that set the prices of its products early in the year to have the prices available to print in catalog mailers. One year there was a mad cow disease scare, as well as an increase in dairy prices that, taken together, increased the organization's purchase price for beef and cheese.

The company faced a huge dilemma. The catalogs were already printed with the prices based on the previous year's costs and sales. On the one hand, they could stick with the prices quoted in the catalogue and not make a profit, due to the costs they would have to incur. On the other hand, they could re-run the catalogs and lose money on the printing costs. Neither was a favorable option. The organization missed seeing the main cost drivers for their products: the price of beef due to the mad cow scare, as well as record high dairy prices that affected their cheese purchases.

In the end the company decided to wait on their purchases of beef and cheese (which was also risky because of order quantities and delivery schedules). Management hoped that the prices of the products would come down as the market shifted and got back in line with how it had been in previous years. That decision actually proved to work in the firm's favor, and it taught management a valuable lesson on paying more attention to the market drivers, as well as timing purchases accordingly.

A second principle is that the indicators and their measures must be easy to understand, and they need to be consistent across the organization. If managers do not clearly see how the measures relate to meeting their organization's objectives, they are unlikely to take action based on them. Moreover, if the units in the organization measure things differently or inconsistently, then the business will eventually become unmanageable. In his white paper, Sacerdote provided an apt example of the problem of inconsistency by using an organization with multiple service centers, each of which measured service quality differently:

> Each of its service centers reported that it was working very efficiently with high quality, but a rising tide of customer complaints, including withheld payments totaling hundreds of millions of dollars, suggested otherwise. Corporate would publish a monthly operations analysis of its service centers that contained hundreds of measures of service efficiency and effectiveness. At any given time, some of these measures were likely to be giving good readings, whence each department's high performance claims. However, these measures were totally disconnected from both the next department's metrics and the customer's experience, so that no one saw the order quality problem except the Collections Department, which received a monthly beating from the CFO for letting receivables get out of control. And, because Collections was constantly in the CFO's doghouse, no one paid any attention to their complaints about order quality problems upstream from them.[5]

Sacerdote concluded by saying, "If the leading indicators are to have any value, managers must understand immediately what to do when a key measure veers off its intended trajectory. If it takes months of analysis and committee meetings to decide what to do, the competitive advantage of having a good set of leading indicators is totally dissipated."[6]

Every organization has multiple drivers of problems related to its market competitiveness. However, choosing appropriate measures of those indicators is no small feat, particularly since many managers have a tendency to focus on one large one (usually a lagging indicator, like revenue growth, market share, or employee turnover) and get blindsided by other factors to which they were not paying particular attention (like service quality or employee grievances), but which have the potential to signal declines in revenue or increases in costs.

The last principle, then, is to choose a small set of the chief leading indicators that are commonly understood by employees across the organization. Interestingly, psychologists claim that most people cannot focus on more than five to seven things at a time. We see this with many of the numbers in our lives, such as five-digit zip codes and seven-digit phone numbers. We suggest that the chosen set of indicators includes no more than seven measures. These should reflect the ability of all employees and units in the organization to see clearly how they affect, and are affected by, the indicators so that they are able to respond quickly in making adjustments to keep competitive.

In essence, without a learning orientation an organization cannot hope to remain competitive. To help with understanding and anticipating an organization's market competitiveness, here is a summary of how you can assist in establishing a learning approach for your organization:

1. Meet with top managers in the organization to understand the specific overall outcomes and results they expect, and identify no more than seven leading indicators that provide information about the progress toward those outcomes.

2. Meet with managers of each primary unit in the organization to establish the five to seven specific leading indicators that signal positive and negative results for their respective units. Make sure that these indicators are consistent and aligned with the overall organizational indicators identified in the first step.

3. Establish understandable and trackable measures for each of the leading indicators (overall organization and sub-units), along with a timetable for when they are measured.

4. Develop easy-to-understand training for how the indicators operate, establish a regular process for reporting their progress toward the desired outcomes and results, and provide graphic representation and clear summaries of each measure to employees.

Source #2: Competency and Distrust

At the end of Chapter 2, we stated that competitive advantage begins with the issue of competency and trust among the organization's members. Reducing uncertainty by involving all organizational members in a learning environment will help, but it is not the only way to foster trust. Remember that, when all is said and done, the employees are the keepers and users of the knowledge gained through the learning that takes place. Therefore, the necessity of having competent, trusting, and trustworthy managers and employees cannot be overstated.

As the quotation from one of the respondents at the beginning of this chapter noted, the uncertainty that is created by market fluctuations and the fear that both managers and employees feel as a result of that uncertainty, tends to spur management decisions that seem arbitrary to employees. When that happens, trust is eroded.

Consider, for example, the frequent downsizing that has occurred over the last decade. In many organizations the culprit was the misprocessing or denial of critical information at a time when the organization had the ability to make incremental changes. Moreover, decisions on who goes and who stays are often made haphazardly or inconsistently.[7] It is no wonder that employees and other stakeholders view downsizing decisions with some skepticism and mistrust. As Hemingway and Conte argued,

> Fairness is an issue during downsizing efforts because of the multiple decisions made by management in determining how many workers to terminate, who to lay off, and how to execute the layoffs. Each of these decisions, if improperly implemented, has the potential to cause both victims and survivors to perceive the entire layoff process as unfair.[8]

But downsizing decisions are not the only ones viewed with uncertainty; any decision that appears to employees that managers are distorting or avoiding reality (that is, critical information) signals incompetency and, subsequently, erodes trust.

A president and CEO used to field questions all the time about his company being sold, the headquarters being relocated, etc. He was good about having monthly town hall meetings. He didn't use any notes, and he allowed for questions at the end. Employees were impressed that he didn't cancel the meetings and that he not only allowed for questions, but he answered them. He was also wise not to make any promises. When employees asked if the company was going to lay off people, for example, he would say, "I must say that we are not planning a reduction in force at this time." When the next month's town hall came, he would be forthright and say, "Last month, someone asked a question about layoffs. I indicated we were not planning to do staff reductions then, but with our latest sales projections, we are going to have to look for ways to cut costs, and our largest expense is our payroll." He assured everyone that if the company did have to reduce staff, everything possible would be done to help them find new jobs and to provide a severance package so they weren't suddenly left without an income. Employees would come together and offer suggestions of how to save money to their managers and to human resources. The employees really rallied behind their company leader because they trusted him, since he always kept his word.

Later, the same company was sold to private equity investors. A new president assumed the leadership of the company. However, this president did not hold town hall meetings, and if someone came to his office, he would have his secretary make up an excuse so he wouldn't be available to address any direct questions that made him uncomfortable. When he got cornered with a question he didn't want to answer, he stumbled over his words and said what he thought the questioner wanted to hear, whether it was true or not. So, when the same layoff question was posed to the new president, he denied that it was even a possibility. Two weeks later, there were massive layoffs. Needless to say, he quickly lost employees' trust and never regained it.

What Affects Trust and Trustworthiness?

Edward Glaeser and his colleagues defined trust as the "commitment of resources to an activity where the outcome depends upon the cooperative behavior of others," and they define trustworthiness as "behavior that increases the returns to people who trust you."[9] One interesting finding in their study was that how much a person trusts others is a significant predictor of how much that person should be trusted. Moreover, they found that the more contact one has with another person, the more that trust—and, thus, trustworthiness—increases between them.

The operating mechanism seems to be in dealing with, not avoiding, critical information. This makes having crucial conversations with employees, no matter how unpleasant the topics may be, necessary for establishing the basis for trust. But it does not mean that the conversation is one-way; in other words, when employees are entrusted with critical information, they feel empowered to help solve organizational problems.

For learning organizations and, specifically, for those organizations that have established or are in the process of designing leading indicators to provide critical market information, trust facilitates the sharing of information.[10] This happens for several reasons, but one important reason for our purposes is that the more honest communication employees have with managers, the more credible and, therefore, the more trustworthy, the manager appears. Of course, it works both ways to create competence-based trust between managers and employees.

The HR director of a promotional marketing company was privy to the fact that her company was getting ready to close one of its locations. Although the announcement hadn't been made public, she knew the closure was forthcoming. A few days before the public announcement, an employee approached her for advice. He had been considering the purchase of a new home and was getting ready to make an offer. However, knowing that other company locations had been closing, he was afraid the same thing would happen to his location. As the sole income earner in a house of four, he didn't want to buy the house if he would soon lose his job. He asked the HR director if there was any indicator that a closure might happen.

Knowing that nothing could be shared, but wanting to help this co-worker of almost eight years, the HR director put herself in his shoes and said that she would probably wait to see what information would be forthcoming at the company meeting the following week. When the announcement was made at the meeting, he thanked her for suggesting that he wait. Although the news was devastating, he was grateful that he didn't make the biggest purchase of his life a week prior to hearing he was going to lose his job.

The availability of managers to provide critical information is also a predictor of how trustworthy they are. When a manager is available for assistance, even if this availability is not acted on, it signals to employees that the manager is more approachable and, therefore, someone who cares about employees and would look out for their interests.[11] In addition, the ability to listen closely signals that a manager is willing to sacrifice time to talk with employees about their problems and concerns. Likewise, employees who listen well are perceived to be engaged in advancing the welfare of the organization and to have the commitment to solving problems that affect it.

Finally, the issues of trust and trustworthiness, as sources of market competitiveness, are extended to the reputation of the overall organization. Dr. Leslie Gaines-Ross, chief reputation strategist at Weber Shandwick, believes that

> The bedrock of corporate reputation is trust. Trust is the oxygen that allows reputation to exist. Without it, reputations would suffer. Trust is all about credibility and, without credibility, reputation does not stand a chance of being built. Today, reputations are built on the belief that a company will do the right thing, treat its employees well, build safe products, deliver on its promises, and will be well governed.[12]

Trusted organizations can attract better business partners, drive premium pricing, hire top employees, and receive the benefit of the doubt in a crisis. They are more likely to have the freedom to operate in the way they choose. Their business is more likely to be sustainable through good cycles and bad because their stakeholders trust them. In essence, establishing trust with those inside and outside the organization helps promote learning, encourages information sharing, and, ultimately, reduces uncertainty and fear.

Attaining Market Competitiveness

Admittedly, market competitiveness is no small problem; if an organization is not competitive, it will ultimately go out of business in the environment in which it operates. However, if we look at the problem of becoming or remaining competitive from the viewpoint of sustainability, what we come to realize is that there really is only one source that will give an organization truly sustainable competitive advantage: its human capital. Despite the lip service paid to this philosophy by many managers, most do not know how to actually put that source to work to create and sustain competitive advantage for their organizations. We provide one example of how you, in your own organization, can help make this happen and help resolve yet another persistent business problem.

Sample Solution #2: Creating a Learning Orientation for Gathering and Using Market Information Expediently

Two sources of problems in becoming or remaining market competitive have to do with (a) not having a learning orientation across the organization and (b) lacking competent, trusting, and trustworthy organizational managers and employees. In Chapter 6, we will deal specifically with employee and managerial competency. But first, we provide some guidelines for establishing a learning process for a specific market competitiveness problem: expediently using social media information about our customers. Don't forget that this is merely an example; we would expect that you will be able to use this as a guide to address a specific market competitiveness problem or issue in your organization (by the way, we have assumed in our example that there are identified leading indicators for your organization's market competitiveness; if these are not already chosen, they will need to be determined before undertaking the steps described in the textbox below).

Step 1: *Choose one critical leading indicator of your organization's market competitiveness as the primary focus.*

For our purposes here, let's say it is "number of social media postings about your organization by month."

Step 2: *Do some preliminary research on how this indicator (driver) is affecting your market competitiveness.*

Obviously, there are many social media outlets, and your organization will need to determine which ones mention your organization or its products/services. There are obvious ones (for example, Facebook, Foursquare, Twitter), but don't forget review sites, like Yelp or the Better Business Bureau, which may have customer review information on your products or services.

To do some preliminary research, use a search engine to search for your organization's name, the name(s) of your products or services, the names of your organization's officers/top managers, and any other keywords that occur to you. The purpose is to get a sense of how the public views your brand, your products and services, and the people who are the "face" of your company. If you don't have much of a Web presence after doing your research, this could be a good thing (no obvious complaints or negative issues), but it could also be a bad thing for your market competitiveness (no helpful comments or positive customer reviews).

Step 3: *Convene a small group of employees to evaluate the nature and source of the information (for example, customers, vendors, internal departments or personnel, market research firm, Better Business Bureau), as well as how current the information is.*

You may wish to adjust the composition of the small group of employees to include other appropriate employees and managers to systematically review the information and report back on what is being learned. Have the group develop the following:

- Analysis of the main complaint, issue, problem, or successful behavior(s) and outcome(s). One helpful way to accomplish this is to rank order the information by number of comments/reviews about the specific issue. If there are not many, this approach is obviously not necessary. Whatever the number, the main information should be phrased in behavioral or outcome terms: for example, "Customer service representative cut off the customer when he or she was speaking (behavior), which resulted in the customer canceling his or her order (outcome)."

- A means to feed back the information to those directly involved, including first-line employees (for example, salespeople, customer service representatives, human resources, safety committee, manufacturing, nurses) and managers. For example, comments about the rudeness or helpfulness of customer service representatives should go to all of them and to any managers responsible for customer service, which might include both a customer service manager and a sales manager. The feedback might be in the form of a brief weekly or monthly report. The timing of such feedback is crucial, however. If a monthly report is used, the same error could be made multiple times before the employee is even aware he or she is making the error. In cases where timeliness is necessary, managers should provide feedback sooner rather than later. Make sure that it clearly identifies the behaviors and outcomes that are essential to know and, if necessary, to change. The feedback should also be written so that the employees will understand it. This means writing at an appropriate literacy level. Everyone writes differently, and all employees have different levels of education. Many organizations encourage managers to use the "readability" level feature in Microsoft Word. We suggest writing most general information at no higher than an eighth-grade reading level so that the greatest number of employees will comprehend what is being said.

- A process for a review and analysis of the feedback. Some of you may be aware that the army conducts what it refers to as an "After-Action Review" (AAR).13 At its core, the AAR is a problem-solving process. The purpose is for participants to discuss what happened, discover strengths and weaknesses in how it occurred, propose solutions, and adopt a course of action to correct problems. The AAR is candid and professional, focusing on performance against the standards for the tasks required. Everyone can, and should, participate if he or she has an insight, observation, or question that will help identify and correct deficiencies or maintain strengths. Be aware that an AAR is not a critique of individual performance; it presumes that no one has all the answers. Therefore, it benefits everyone by allowing all team members to learn from each other.

For business organizations, an AAR can be just as valuable as it is for the army because it allows for an honest discussion, without assigning blame, so that problems can be addressed and information can be shared with everyone concerned. In the case of rudeness of customer service personnel in our running example, the following steps should occur:

1. Provide a full description of the complaint, and identify the specific behaviors, outcomes, and context that the group will be addressing.

2. Ask appropriate questions that arrive at the process of what happened. As the HR pro-

fessional, it makes sense that you act as the facilitator and guide the review using a logical sequence of events to describe and discuss what happened. Do not ask yes or no questions, but encourage participation and guide discussion by using open-ended questions that have no specific answer and that allow the person answering to reply based on what was significant to him or her. Open-ended questions are less likely to put someone on the defensive. For example, it is better to ask, "What happened after the customer said she wanted to return the blouse?" as opposed to, "Why did you cut off the customer on the phone?"

3.   Be specific, avoid generalizations, and focus on behaviors, not the person actually engaging in the behaviors. Also, keep bringing the discussion back to how the performance under discussion affects what the organization is trying to achieve.

4.   Continually summarize where the group is in the process, what it has already decided, and which decisions it still has left to make.

•   Suggestions for improving and changing the process, structure, system, quality, operating procedures, speed, or whatever is needed. Following the sharing of the critical market information and its analysis, the group can suggest changes so that the potential problem is less likely to recur. Again, gathering market competitiveness information is only beneficial if changes are made as a result. Identify ideas that can help avoid the issue in the future. Bring everyone into the idea discussion, and consider how each idea will or will not help solve the problem. Even if a member has no idea to contribute, he or she can still provide evaluation information.

As the Roosevelt quotation that began this chapter noted, co-operation begins where competition leaves off. As a leader in your company, one of your jobs is to engage employees cooperatively in helping the organization manage and resolve its problems. The second common business problem—market competitiveness—may seem as if it is out of your wheelhouse. But helping establish a learning orientation so that critical market information is not only available but is also used to reduce uncertainty and fear can set you apart from the crowd. The key to remember about this technique is that it is really about training employees (and managers, for that matter) on the drivers of profit and cost so that everyone understands. Ultimately, however, building a learning orientation is about fostering trust and competency within your organization so that the fundamental problems are not ignored, and the information about those problems is gathered and responded to in time to make a difference.

Common Business Problem #3: *Ad Quod Damnum**: How Do We Deal with All the Changing Laws and Regulations?

"People crushed by laws have no hope but to evade power. If the laws are their enemies, they will be enemies to the law; and those who have most to hope and nothing to lose will always be dangerous."

—*Edmund Burke*

We have already stated that critical problems become catastrophic when organizations cannot adapt quickly enough, and this is particularly difficult with changes in legislation and government regulations. Often the difficulty rests in our interpretation of the law or regulation with regard to our specific organizations, and not necessarily in our ability to adapt to it. In other words, before we can know what to do, we have to know what it truly means for our organizations, and this could entail both benefits and harms.

We could list a host of well-publicized "the sky is falling" fears for large and small organizations across the nation, but let's just look at one example. In 2006, Ohio voters approved an amendment to the state constitution setting the state's minimum wage at $6.85 an hour with a built-in increase attached to infla-

---

* *Latin legal term meaning, "according to the harm."*

tion each year. Governor Robert Taft signed the bill into law in 2007. Interestingly, that same year President George W. Bush also signed a bill raising the federal minimum wage. Both state and federal increases to the minimum wage set off a firestorm from businesspersons who vowed they would have to close their doors because they would not be able to pay their employees. This reaction also occurred in 2009, and is poised to occur again, as President Barack Obama has suggested that the federal minimum wage should increase substantially by 2015.[1]

But here are two facts about what historically has happened to employment and organizational well-being after raising the minimum wage:

1. The preponderance of research suggests that even during hard economic times, raising the minimum wage does not reduce employment.[2] Usually increases in compensation of low-wage workers reduces turnover and increases demand for goods and services. These positive aspects help provide needed revenue for the businesses that are expending more in wages, thereby balancing out any potential negative financial effects—and this includes small businesses. In fact, for over six years (1997-2003) small business retail employment grew three times more (9.2 percent) in higher minimum wage states than in low minimum wage states (3.0 percent).[3]

2. More businesses close because of poor management than because of increased employee wages. According to the annual Dun & Bradstreet survey, the most common causes of business failure are management incompetence (46 percent) and a lack of management experience (30 percent).[4] Therefore, it is more likely that management problems have led to an inability to generate revenue to pay employees, rather than the wages (that is, increased costs) themselves causing organizational failures.

The reality is that less than 1 percent of organizations fail to remain viable because of state or federally mandated wage increases.[5] This brief example demonstrates that managers are often fearful and opposed to changes in laws and regulations, even when they have no factual basis for those fears.

A Real Fear: Employee Lawsuits!

Among the prevailing fears about laws and regulations in organizations, a real one has to do with lawsuits—particularly those from applicants, employees, or former employees. Here are some interesting facts about employee lawsuits:

- Organizations almost always lose lawsuits that stem from retaliation. Judges and juries are especially tough when they perceive that a manager reacted inappropriately when an employee filed a complaint about being discriminated against or being treated unfairly.
- If the case goes to a jury, age or disability discrimination claims will cost an organization the most money to defend.
- The most common lawsuit filed against organizations remains sex or race discrimination.[6]
- The U.S. Department of Labor (DOL) estimates that approximately 70 percent of employers routinely violate wage and hour laws; for example, the DOL Wage and Hour Division recovered back wages of $1.4 billion for fiscal years 2001 through 2008, with numbers continuing to grow in 2010 and beyond.[7]

According to the website for InsurePro, a specialty firm providing professional liability insurance coverage for a variety of businesses,

Companies are finding that they are vulnerable from the pre-hiring process through the exit interview, even if the employee was never hired, or only at the company a matter of days. . . . Every employer faces the reality that it will be the target of legal action from past, present and prospective employees. Even if the claim is groundless or fraudulent, the defense of a suit can be expensive in time, resources and financially.[8]

Many organizations do have business liability insurance, but it may surprise you to learn that business liability insurance only covers *financial* liability. If an employee claims his or her legal rights have been violated, most workers' compensation laws and general liability insurance policies exclude employment-related exposure. As a result, most organizations are vulnerable to employee lawsuits, and that is why we recommend employment practices liability insurance (EPLI). Such coverage includes any financial liability that may be incurred as a result of employment litigation, including expenses related to the organization's legal defense.

What Are the Benefits of EPLI?

In 1998, two Supreme Court cases established that supervisors and managers are, in fact, extensions of the company.[9] In 2013, the Supreme Court in *Vance v. Ball State University*, provided a new definition for what constitutes a "supervisor" or "management-level employee": that is, those employees who "are empowered to take tangible employment actions against lower-level employees, such as having the authority to hire and fire."[10] Therefore, for employees claiming discrimination, harassment, or other mistreatment, an employer is automatically ("strictly") liable *unless* the following occur:

- The employer took reasonable measures to prevent the adverse actions from occurring in the first place through proper policy, proper complaint procedure, and training.
- The organization promptly corrected the behavior(s) once it was reported.

- The employee unreasonably failed to take advantage of preventive and corrective opportunities provided by the employer.

For organizations that want to protect themselves against managers and supervisors who act inappropriately, EPLI can provide protection against sexual harassment, discrimination, wrongful termination, breach of employment contract, negligent evaluation, libel, slander, failure to employ, promote/grant tenure, wrongful discipline, deprivation of career opportunity, wrongful infliction of emotional distress, mismanagement of employee benefits plans, whistle-blower and retaliation claims, invasion of privacy, wage and hour claims, as well as other employment-related claims.

One major advantage to EPLI is that it covers claims made not only by current employees but also by former or prospective employees who might charge that they were victims of employment-related discrimination on the basis of any federal, state, or local law that prohibits discrimination. EPLI may also be combined with liability insurance that protects against claims that allege misconduct by the officers or directors of a company against individuals or groups. What makes EPLI interesting is that these policies are custom-made for each organization's needs, and they also cover unintentional violations. However, they do not usually cover punitive damages or civil and criminal penalties or liabilities covered by other insurance, such as workers' compensation.

Another benefit to purchasing an EPLI policy is that most insurers will review and make recommendations to add or amend employment practices before insuring the company.[11] This is especially beneficial to new and smaller companies that may not have proper employment practices in place.

The bottom line is that the costs of litigating a single-plaintiff employment case have been estimated at somewhere between $100,000 and $200,000 or, in some cases, more.[12] Clearly, in an organization of any size, the need for protection against real or fraudulent lawsuits and claims has never been greater.

What Are the Costs of EPLI?

EPLI costs are determined by the size of a company, the number of employees, the type of industry, reputation, length of time in business, claims history, risk profile, selection processes, termination procedures, employee turnover rates, the amount of coverage needed, and whether the organization chooses to have coverage for potential third-party claims, such as inappropriate behavior by customers and vendors. Most small- and medium-sized businesses can expect to pay premiums of between $800 and $3,000 annually (depending on the factors just mentioned). Typical EPLI limit options are $25,000, $50,000, $75,000, $100,000, and $250,000 with deductibles varying between $5,000 and $25,000. Defense costs are included within the specific policy's "limit of liability," that is, the limit that is reached by a total of both defense costs and indemnity payments.

When compared to the cost of litigation, even if the employer wins, EPLI may be worth the investment. Attorneys fees alone can be astronomical. A company has to weigh the risk of not having EPLI. It would probably pay for itself with just one defended lawsuit.

However, this type of insurance is not that well known. One attorney we spoke with said that "even though I have practiced employment law for several years, I have never encountered a defendant with EPLI before, and I didn't even realize that it was available."

Why might this be?

One reason is that many companies choose to settle out of court, primarily to avoid the bad press that often accompanies lawsuits, particularly those filed by employees. Unfortunately, the more employers are willing to settle out of court, the more likely we will see an increase in lawsuits, primarily because employees feel confident that they will get some money out of a lawsuit. It's rather like playing the lottery—choosing to file lawsuits in the hopes of getting a settlement.

With the changing laws and regulations that most organizations experience employers need a better solution to help protect themselves against employee lawsuits and the financial uncertainty they bring. Even a frivolous claim can cost an employer tens of thousands of dollars in attorney fees. As the legal challenge of employee lawsuits continues to rise, HR leaders would be wise to recommend EPLI to their employers.

We Have to Do What and by When?

Organizations also run into difficulties when passage of a law or regulation occurs without much time for preparation, and the law may not be fully understood, even by the legislative or regulatory bodies that have introduced it. Part of the organization-environment fit problem in this case is the ability to adapt quickly enough so that the misalignment between the environment and your organization is minimized.

One such example is the relatively new law that was mentioned often in our study as one of the most feared and anticipated by a majority of the respondents: the Patient Protection and Affordable Care Act (the PPACA, which is often abbreviated as ACA, and it is also colloquially referred to as "Obamacare"). Let's review what this law actually requires of organizations, inasmuch as we are able to figure out at the present time, and examine why everyone is so afraid of it.

What the PPACA Requires of U.S. Organizations

This law is extensive—no question about that; however, with regard to many businesses and organizations, it may be less scary than one might imagine. One reason is that for most large organizations not much will change regarding their health care offerings.

The prediction has been that fully 94 percent of organizations with at least 50 employees should experience no change in their health care benefits offerings.[13] However, as we write this, there has been and continues to be confusion among organizations about which policies meet or do not meet the standards required of the law. As a result, many employees are experiencing policy cancellations—some legitimately based on the law and others due to ignorance about what the law really requires.

Following are some of the main requirements that directly affect most organizations, particularly those that managers think will pose critical problems for their organizations. We first provide the basics of the law, followed by our basic interpretation (again, insofar as we know at the time of this writing) of what it means for most organizations.

Limits on Group Health Plans

There cannot be lifetime limits or unreasonable annual limits on the dollar value of benefits for participants or beneficiaries. Moreover, the benefits cannot discriminate in favor of highly compensated employees. The insurance company cannot rescind coverage once the participant has been accepted into the plan, nor can it refuse coverage to employees based on preexisting health conditions. Additionally, the waiting period to begin an employee's coverage cannot exceed 90 days.

What this means in plain language: Health insurers can no longer limit the dollar value paid out to an insured person or that person's beneficiaries. So, if the insured gets a lifetime chronic disease or has a premature baby with health problems, and it ends up costing the insurer millions of dollars, so be it. Additionally, a person cannot be turned down for coverage because of a preexisting disease or condition and, once insured, the person's coverage cannot be discontinued by the insurer. Finally, the maximum number of days any employee must wait before coverage starts is 90 days.

Affordability of Coverage

Employers must, at a minimum, provide coverage for recommended immunizations, well-baby care, and annual breast cancer screenings for women. If an employer charges employees premiums of more than 9.8 percent of a worker's family income, or if the employer pays less than 60 percent of the total premium, the worker may enroll in the insurance exchange for his or her state. Organizations may use an employee's wages from Box 1 on the W-2 to establish the affordability of employee coverage. A tax credit will also assist small businesses with fewer than 25 workers with up to 50 percent of the total premium cost. Employers with more than 200 employees must automatically enroll new full-time employees in coverage (full-time means at least 30 hours per week). However, there must be an option for employees to opt out of the automatic coverage, should they choose to do so.

What this means in plain language: The full cost of preventive care for infants, children, and women must be covered by an organization's health insurance plan, including annual screening for cholesterol, diabetes, blood pressure, and several types of cancer, as well as help for employees to quit smoking. The whole point of the PPACA is so that more people will be able to afford to have health insurance. Therefore, every employee working at least 30 hours per week has the option of receiving coverage from his or her employer or, if the premiums charged by the employer exceed 9.8 percent of the employee's family income or the employer pays less than 60 percent of that premium, the employee can opt to join the state or federal insurance exchange pool and receive "premium assistance credits." However, to do that, employees cannot make more than 400 percent of the federal poverty level (which means, for a family of four, they cannot make more than about $92,000/year). Premium assistance credits, which are refundable and payable by the Internal Revenue Service (IRS) in advance directly to the insurer, subsidize the purchase of health insurance plans through a state or federal marketplace (also known as an "exchange"). The employee then pays to the plan in which he or she is enrolled the dollar difference between the premium assistance credit amount and the total premium charged for the plan. For employed individuals who purchase health insurance through an exchange, the premium payments are made through payroll deductions from the employer. Small employers (fewer than 25 employees) will receive a tax credit for 50 percent of their employees' premium costs.

Penalties for Noncompliance

Any employer with at least 50 full-time employees (work more than 30 hours per week) that does not offer coverage and has at least one full-time employee receiving the premium assistance credit will make a penalty payment of $2,000 per full-time employee. An employer with more than 50 employees that offers coverage that is deemed unaffordable or does not meet the standard for minimum essential coverage, but has at least one full-time employee receiving the premium assistance tax credit (because the coverage is either unaffordable or the employer does not cover 60 percent of total costs), will pay the lesser of $3,000 for each of those employees receiving the credit or $750 for each of their full-time employees.

What this means in plain language: Any organization employing 50 or more employees will be penalized if it (a) decides not to offer coverage, (b) offers coverage that costs above 9.8 percent of employees' family income, (c) doesn't pay at least 60 percent of the total premium costs, or (d) offers coverage that doesn't meet the minimum essential coverage and has at least one employee who works 30 hours or more who has opted out and is eligible to receive premium assistance because of his or her wages falling below 400 percent of the federal poverty level. In other words, not complying with the law will cost an organization, at the least, $3,000 for the one uncovered employee and, at the most, $750 per every employee who works 30 hours or more, whether the rest of them are covered or not.

Extension of Benefits to Children Up to 26-Years-Old

Health coverage for an employee's unmarried children until the month they attain 26 years of age is tax-free to the employee. This allows employers with cafeteria plans to permit employees to make pretax contributions to pay for this expanded benefit. This benefit also applies to self-employed individuals. The limit on pretax contributions to a health savings account, however, will be $2,500.

What this means in plain language: Employees or self-employed persons can keep their children on their employer's health plan through the end of the month that the children turn 26. Pretax dollars (up to $2,500) can be used to pay into health savings accounts or other employer-sponsored plans for these children, just as they had been doing all along for the rest of their families.

Reporting of Benefits

The act requires employers to report the cost of coverage under an employer-sponsored group health plan. This reporting is for informational purposes only, to show employees the value of their health care benefits so they can be more informed consumers. Therefore, it must be in understandable language and be restricted to four pages or less for the employees of that organization. The amount reported does not affect tax liability, as the value of the employer contribution to health coverage continues to be excludible from an employee's income, and it is not taxable. Any employer failing to comply with the reporting aspect is fined $1,000 per failure (calculated by multiplying $1,000 by the number of employees who failed to receive the report).

What this means in plain language: Employers should annually provide a written statement to each employee that details the benefits received, what the employer paid for them, and their value to the employee. If an employer doesn't report said benefits to employees, the employer will be fined $1,000 for each employee not so informed. In other words, if an organization with 60 employees doesn't provide a statement of benefits to any of them, that organization will end up paying a $60,000 fine!

Excise Tax on High-Cost Employer-Sponsored
Health Coverage

The PPACA levies a new excise tax of 40 percent on insurance companies and plan administrators for any health coverage plan with an annual premium that is above the statutory limit of $10,200 for single coverage and $27,500 for family coverage.[14] The tax applies to self-insured plans and plans sold in the group market, and for coverage eligible for the deduction for self-employed individuals. The tax applies to the amount of the premium in excess of the threshold.

What this means in plain language: The PPACA is designed to eliminate inequity in health insurance plans and to lower how much people use their health insurance. Therefore, the excise tax discourages employers from purchasing plans that are over the statutory limit by making the next dollar 40 percent more expensive. This could be quite expensive for those organizations that provide over-the-top coverage to key employees or senior managers.

What Do Employers Fear Most about the PPACA?

Interestingly, if you really look at the main requirements for organizations, the biggest fears and worries can be grouped into three categories: (a) the process of compliance, (b) the cost of compliance, and (c) the cost of noncompliance. Organizations must make sure they are enrolling and covering employees correctly, and they must be prepared to pay for the coverage, at least at the levels the law requires, or be penalized.

To summarize the "process" category, an organization must provide health care coverage for its full-time employees (or full-time equivalent employees) if it has 50 or more who work 30 hours or more per week and must cover dependents until they are 26. Moreover, the employer must make sure those employees are informed of their options in language that they can understand, and new employees must be enrolled as soon as they join the organization or, at least, no more than 90 days after they begin work. The organization cannot provide inequitable benefits based on salary or wages. It cannot refuse coverage based on any preexisting health condition or status, and it must report those benefits and their value each year to employees. This surely doesn't sound like rocket science, does it? These process fears are generally unfounded, given that most carriers will make sure that the organizations they cover are following these mandates.

The costs of noncompliance are based on not doing the above things, and organizations are wise not to test the limits, or they will incur penalties. Unfortunately, without understanding all the ramifications, the various penalties give businesses a powerful incentive to downsize their staffs to fewer than 50 full-time equivalent workers, replace full-time employees with part-timers who work fewer than 30 hours per week, and contract out work to other firms or individuals. In this case, the benefits of noncompliance appear to outweigh the costs of compliance. However, notice that the law says "full-time equivalent" workers, not 50 employees. Thus, downsizing for many organizations will not solve the problem they fear. These subtleties notwithstanding, the costs of compliance seem to concern our survey respondents the most. To anticipate these costs, as with the other business problems discussed in this book, we need some indicators for them.

What Are Potential Indicators?

As we have already discussed, monitoring critical information is key to adapting our organizational response to various environments. The choice of indicators that signal changes in an organization's environment *and* our adaptations to it are crucial to how well we weather the health insurance requirement changes in our firms—no matter what our size or situation.

Part of the critical information we need to have at our fingertips has to do with changing workforce demographics, the use of technology in health care delivery and systems, and the overall support and encouragement provided to employees for maintaining their health. However, another crucial part also has to do with being able to get a handle on how the benefits you already provide are being used. Performing a *utilization review* can give an organization some understanding of how its benefits are being used, or even if they are being used, by employees. The results of the review can inform our choices of what to retain, change, or add into our current plans.

Conducting a Utilization Review

The purpose of a benefits utilization review is to determine which benefits employees are actually using. Knowing the frequency and to what extent a particular benefit is used may help your organization determine cost-saving practices, as well as which benefits are actually creating the results you seek for your employees. For medical plans, the insurer can usually provide a utilization review for you.

There are several parts to the utilization review process. To begin, we suggest that you review the organizational strategy to develop some goals for what your organization is trying to achieve with its benefits offerings. For example, do you attempt to attract and retain employees through attractive benefits, rather than pay larger salaries? Are you more concerned with offering benefits that target a particular demographic (for example, child care for people with young children versus elder care for older employees who have aging parents) or benefits that have broad appeal to all groups of employees? In your organization are benefits considered part of total compensation or an add-on to other monetary rewards and incentives? Questions such as these will help you initially determine how to approach benefits restructuring (or offering them for the first time) so that they align with the organization's strategic goals.

Along with the strategic questions are the monetary questions because, obviously, your organization has limited funds to spend on benefits. Therefore, the second step is to analyze current benefits costs and create a budget that outlines annual benefits cost projections. As certain benefits are becoming more expensive—like health insurance, in particular—your organization will likely have to curtail other benefits. But this is precisely why a utilization analysis is so valuable. You certainly don't want to offer costly benefits if only a few employees are using them. On the other hand, some benefits have low cost, and providing them to employees may be worth it for motivational and commitment purposes, even if only a few people use them.

Additionally, conducting an anonymous survey of employees would help you see which of the myriad benefits you offer are liked and are used by employees. A simple survey is all that is generally necessary to gauge how well the benefits you currently offer meet the needs of the employees. But beware! If you ask employees how well they like the benefits you provide and their feedback indicates changes are needed, the motivation and trust that asking them provided will be lost if you don't make the changes. If you decide not to make the changes or additions they've suggested, be sure to give them an honest reason why.

Most important in a utilization review, however, is objective data that show which benefits are being used and which are rarely used, as well as the costs associated with each. For health insurance, hospitalization, dental care, eye care, and other medical benefits, your insurance carrier should be able to provide you with data that details the use for each benefit offered. These data do not identify specific employees, but give you totals across all employees—what is known as "metadata." Some carriers have the capability to break these data down even further by age, sex, and marital/family status, which would also be helpful to know for planning purposes. However, even nonmedical benefits such as educational assistance or reimbursement, paid time off, and 401(k) or 403(b) contributions should be tallied to note the spectrum of use and their associated costs.

All in all, conducting a benefits utilization review is a smart thing for organizations to do at least every few years. It will help allay some of the fear for managers if they know that the choices they make are ones that employees will support, too. Moreover, having the critical information will help your organization adapt more quickly to changes that are sure to occur as legislation in health care marches on. In addition, because the PPACA requires you to report the benefits employees receive each year, a utilization review will give you ready access to the data to do exactly that.

In our "sample solution" section for this chapter we discuss how you and your employees can become engaged in changing the culture of your organization from one that does nothing to encourage (or one that perhaps even punishes) healthy lifestyles to one that engages all employees in supporting everyone's health and well-being. From a strategic perspective, this will be one of the best approaches to lowering health care costs, specifically, as well as to increase the morale, productivity, and commitment of employees, generally—in other words, together you can create a wellness culture that can literally change lives!

Wellness and the PPACA

Wellness strategy has, and continues to be, a centerpiece of the PPACA.[15] The act expands, in some ways, the incentives that can be used to drive wellness. Employers can now offer increased incentives to employees for participation in a wellness program or for meeting certain health status targets. The law permits organizations to reward employees with premium discounts of up to 30 percent of the cost of health coverage. On the other hand, it also allows employers to penalize employees the same amount for refusing to participate in wellness programs.

And there's more. The PPACA also creates a $200 billion, five-year program to provide grants to small employers (fewer than 100 employees) for comprehensive workplace wellness programs, as long as they did not have a wellness program when the law was enacted. Many smaller, not-for-profit and family-owned businesses can benefit from this grant program.

There is a lot of leeway in how an organization's wellness program is designed, in that it can operate as a participation-only program or as a contingent program. A participation-only program is one based strictly on taking part in the activities and behaviors of the program. Examples of such programs include the following:

- Payment for a fitness center membership.
- A reward for participation in a diagnostic testing program.
- A program for reimbursement of participating in a smoking cessation program.
- A reward for attending monthly no-cost health education seminars.
- A reward for completion of a health risk assessment (HRA).

An outcome-based wellness program requires participants to achieve a specific goal, such as a program that provides rewards for a certain amount of weight lost, actually stopping smoking, or achieving a targeted cholesterol level. In essence, the law can help organizations begin to change their unhealthy culture to one that embraces wellness.

What Do We Mean by a "Health Culture" in Organizations?

Before we detail the steps you and your employees can take to change the health culture in your organization, we should probably clarify what we mean when we say "culture." Organizations, like societies, operate based on rules, policies, laws, and norms. It is this idea of norms that we will mostly deal with here as we talk about organizational culture and, particularly, the culture of health.

To begin, there are several views of organizational culture that have a part to play in shaping how members of that culture think and act. Here are just three of them:

- Culture is a process of "sense-making" in organizations in which the members create a shared understanding about what reality is in their organization, as well as what they value together as a group. In this view culture consists of shared beliefs, attitudes, and values. As a result, *we are what we agree that we are.*

- Culture also consists of consistent, observable patterns of behavior. In this view the basis of culture can be seen in the repeated behaviors or habits enacted by its members. In other words, *we are what we continue to do.*

- Culture is a social control system that promotes and reinforces normative thinking and behaving (that is, the social norms you want employees to have). In this view members are rewarded for doing the "right" things (that is, conforming to the norms that the majority support) and are sanctioned for doing things that stray outside the agreed-on norms. Therefore, *we are what the culture rewards us for being.*

A Word about Norms

Norms are beliefs, shared by a group, about what is context-appropriate behavior. As such, they are extremely important in understanding and predicting people's behavior in the larger society and in organizations. In organizations, cultural norms have influence on which behaviors are easily changed and which are more difficult to change. Implicit here is the idea that established cultural norms can become *impediments* to organizational change, particularly when they are strongly held by a majority of employees. In other words, when there are substantial environmental changes and the members find it difficult to change "how we do things around here," the organization's overall ability to adapt quickly (or at all) is hampered. And, as you might suspect, this inability to adapt subsequently degrades the organization-environment fit. Ultimately, norms likely provide the greatest challenge, but also hold the most promise, for changing behaviors and attitudes in your organization.

With these characteristics firmly in our minds, let's turn to the idea that we can introduce new health and health-related beliefs, attitudes, values, and behaviors, but only if we create shared understanding, new behavioral patterns, and reinforced norms with all members of the organization—including management at all levels. In other words, we must change our organization's health culture before we can facilitate sustainable changes in the actual health of its members.

As we consider the three views of organizational culture described in the previous section, recognize that all three have to be addressed for cultural change to occur. So, to begin the process of moving your organization from unhealthy to healthy, you will need to work on each aspect: (1) creating shared understanding about what it means to be unhealthy and healthy, (2) changing unhealthy behaviors, and (3) reinforcing healthy behavioral norms.

Creating Shared Understanding and Values about Healthy Lifestyles

If people are not aware that they are living unhealthy lives, it is a sure bet that they are not going to change anytime soon. So one of the first things required is to give them the facts. For example, providing health screenings for cholesterol, blood pressure, and glucose levels can provide the baseline information people need. But these also have to be accompanied by what normal levels for these indicators should be for individual employees. Therefore, individual consultations and coaching will be required. To be honest, this process is time-consuming. But it is a crucial first step in creating awareness and a shared understanding of what it means to be unhealthy and what it means to be healthy, as well as what will be required of everyone in the organization.

The Problem with Distortion and Denial

It is not only managers who deny, distort, or tolerate critical problems. On an individual employee level, denial or distortion of information also occurs. People often say, "Yeah, I know I should stop smoking," "I should really stop eating out so much," or "I'm trying to lose weight, but I'm working so much I don't have time to exercise." These distortions and denials must be met with facts about the difficulty in changing behaviors, as well as the incremental nature of what is required to become healthier.

Psychologically, there are three types of denial. The most common type of denial is denial about the causes of the problem. In other words, the employee won't deny that she smokes or is overweight, but she cannot admit or does not realize why. What she does, instead, is to blame her smoking on her addictive personality or her weight gain on her age, neither of which she believes she can overcome, so why bother? This type of denial, ultimately, is a problem of control; in essence, she does not feel in control and, therefore, chooses to attribute the causes to things outside her control. To address this type of denial requires changing beliefs about what someone is or is not in control of.

A second type is denial about the severity of the problem. In our example, this would take the form of minimizing her weight gain: "I'm not that overweight." In many cases this pattern of denial may not be problematic: We all gain and lose weight as a normal part of life. However, if someone gains just five pounds a year (which doesn't seem like a lot), over the course of five years he or she will have gained 25 pounds!

Denial about severity can become a problem in and of itself. Consider that most addictions start out with small behaviors and escalate over time, often without seeming to be a problem for the addicted person (the "I can handle it" denial). By the time people with addictions admit they cannot "handle it," the damage to relationships, as well as to their mental and physical health, may already be done. Addressing one's denial about the severity of a problem requires awareness of one's individual and incremental behaviors and their relationships to unhealthy outcomes.

Which leads us to the third type: denial of the consequences as a result of the problem. In this case of the employee who is overweight, though she again does not deny she has gained weight or that her eating habits are not particularly healthy, she minimizes those problems so that, by association, the outcomes and risks that could be linked with being overweight are also minimized. Perhaps she has missed a lot of work recently or her productivity and job performance have slowly declined over the last few years. This type of denial is a form of association bias—the inability to see that condition A (weight gain) is directly related to outcome B (absenteeism or low productivity at work). Addressing the causal link between one's behaviors and associated outcomes is the key to overcoming this pattern of denial.

Of course, awareness and acceptance of reality are only the beginning. A number of organizations have begun to provide their employees with their health information, but unless it is accompanied by the next important step—training and coaching—it won't mean much.

By training and coaching, we mean training people to *think* differently and then helping them actually to *do* things differently. The training component is crucial in that it must be individualized to each employee. Some employees will jump right on board; others will need to be coaxed along. Many organizations employ outside organizations to help with this.

Coaching means identifying what employees do well and what they might do differently. It begins by developing a trusting and honest relationship with employees, one that recognizes each person's individual situation and ability to change. Remember—we are attempting to change beliefs, attitudes, values, and behaviors here, so it will take some time. Don't expect miracles in a few months.

Changing Patterns of Health Behaviors

Once people are aware and accept the reality of their health status, there are really only three reasons they can't or won't change the way they behave: Either they don't know how (ability), they don't want to change (motivation), or they don't have the resources available to be able to change (support). In most organizations, you'll find a combination of all three. Your approach to creating a culture of health should address all three. Unfortunately, most managers in organizations don't understand or don't want to take the time to approach culture change in the most effective way. Generally, they want to announce a change, implement the change, and move forward, but it is not that simple or easy, because dealing with individual health behaviors requires more than just a mandate to "get healthy."

Creating the Ability to Change

We have already said that training people to think differently is an important step. However, thinking alone will not make people healthier! What is required is giving them the tools and the knowledge to actually change. A lot of this has to do with helping them assess what is realistic for them. For example, if I weigh 300 pounds, it is unrealistic to expect that I will lose half my body weight in one year (an outcome). Not only is that goal unhealthy, but it is also scary for me to think about what I must do to accomplish it, and, as a consequence of that fear, I either won't start a plan or I'll give up before I've reached it. But it is perfectly reasonable to expect that by the end of one year I will be walking three times a week for 30 minutes (a behavior). To overcome inertia we can help employees think about a realistic vision for their behavior. If they can sustain their new behavior, they will ultimately achieve the outcome they wish.

Reinforcing Healthy Norms

Isaac Newton's physics principle that "a body at rest tends to stay at rest; a body in motion tends to stay in motion" can also be figuratively and literally applied to people's motivation to improve their physical health. Most of us can be talked into changing our behaviors for a short time. If you have ever gone to your local gym right after the first of the year, you'll see that it is packed to the gills with people starting an exercise program . . . the power of the New Year's resolution at work! If you continue to go, however, by March or so there is no problem getting on the machines, in the pool, or in a group class. Most of the "resolution" people have abandoned their good intentions in favor of less healthy pursuits. Therefore, the goal of creating a healthy culture is to achieve long-term behavioral change, and that is much harder to do. One truth about organizational change of any sort is that there are several dynamics at work that conspire to stop change in its tracks (see text box). Let's look at how these affect why people have difficulty accepting and embracing change.

Change is tough for many people, primarily because it often makes them feel stupid and incompetent. Even positive or neutral changes can feel awkward. Consider if you were asked to write your signature as you normally would on a check or a legal document. It is probably a no-brainer for you. You do it all the time without even thinking about it. It feels comfortable. But if you were asked to switch hands to your least dominant hand and write your signature, you would feel awkward and silly—even though writing with your other hand certainly isn't a life-and-

---

The Seven Dynamics of Change

1. People will feel awkward and ill at ease.

2. People will think of what they have to give up.

3. People will feel alone, even if others are also going through it.

4. People can only handle so much change at a time.

5. People are at different levels of readiness for change.

6. People will think they don't have enough resources.

7. People will revert to old behavior once the pressure is off.

---

death change. Try it, and you'll see what we mean! That is how change feels to most people who have been doing something the same way for a long time and are then asked to do it differently.

The second dynamic has to do with grieving and loss. When you ask people to radically change their behavior, their situation, or their approach to something, they begin to think of what they are losing, even when they aren't particularly fond of their current behavior or situation. One of Dale's friends who had been with the same company for over 20 years had complained about his job for the last several years—how he hated the hours, his gossipy co-workers, his boss. His wife was offered a transfer to a completely different state, and, after discussing it with her husband, she accepted the offer. Dale saw him shortly after they had moved to the East Coast and was amazed at how he talked constantly about his old company. Even though his most recent experiences were not the best, he was grieving what he had lost by moving east for his wife's job. It doesn't sound rational, does it? But then, people aren't always rational when it comes to their feelings. Effective managers must realize that no matter how positive a change or improvement might appear to them, it may take employees a while to grieve the loss of the old way of doing things before they accept the new way.

A third barrier is somewhat related to the awkward-incompetent dynamic. Sometimes when employees are asked to change something, they believe that they are the only ones in the organization who don't "get" it or who are struggling with the change. They believe that others are not experiencing the same feelings or ineptitude that they are. Of course, this isn't actually true, but the perception for the employee who feels that way is true. It is important for managers to connect people to each other during the process and to encourage them to express their fears.

Everyone has a different tolerance and readiness for change. The fourth and fifth dynamics of change imply that there is no "one size fits all" when it comes to introducing and implementing changes in an organization. These aspects are often the major ones that managers just don't understand and, in the long run, typically cause the overall organizational change to be derailed. The key is to keep the change moving forward while, at the same time, making sure no one is left behind. It is an art, but it is a crucial part of any change effort.

Unfortunately, the sixth barrier is often a true state of affairs in many organizations, not just a perception on the employees' part. Organizations embarking on a change generally do not provide enough resources to actually implement an effective long-term change. Or, if employers do provide resources, they are not distributed to the right people at the right time, thereby wasting them early on in the process or withholding them until it is too late for them to be effective. A great deal of planning is required to know exactly what is needed and when it is needed.

One example of this problem occurred early in the 1990s when a lot of organizations jumped on the Total Quality Management (TQM) bandwagon with great enthusiasm. One of the aspects that seemed to flummox a number of companies was the notion of "self-managed teams." A lot of us in the academic community got flooded with requests to do workshops on team building. Dale remembers being called to do one of these and asking the person on the other end of the phone exactly what had changed in the jobs that now required teams. The company hadn't changed a thing. What the employer wanted, really, was better problem-solving and communication among its workers who, individually, were not particularly good at doing either one. However, the resources needed to actually create these outcomes had already been spent on rolling out the idea of TQM—the organization hosted expensive management retreats to teach managers about TQM, provided training to all employees on how to do statistical process control, and paid to bring in consultants. In essence, there was no money or time left to do the hard work of training people on problem-solving and interpersonal communication and creating the team atmosphere that was needed to pull all of this together to make it work effectively.

Finally, it is critical to make sure that the necessary elements are present to keep employees from reverting to old behaviors. This requires both incentives to continue the new behaviors and consequences for not continuing to act in the new way. This is tricky, since most managers, once the change is considered "done," go on to something new. Unfortunately, without continuing to pay attention to make sure the change has been well established, people will slowly slip into their old ways of doing things. As a point of fact, it takes approximately six months to establish a permanent behavioral change and, during that time, constant reinforcement for the change is required.[16] And, depending on how dramatic the change is, it could take some folks even longer. As an example, if you have been eating sugar-laden foods most of your lives, learning how to avoid those foods and eat raw vegetables for a snack will probably take longer than establishing a 15-minute walking regime as part of your day.

Assessing and Providing Support

It is true that organizations cannot be totally responsible for providing all the necessary reinforcement and support for their employees to attain and maintain healthy lifestyles, but it is also true that many of us spend more time at work than we do at home with friends and family. Recent research has found that the social networks formed at work—formal and informal, online and face-to-face—can play leading roles in influencing people's health behaviors.

Researchers at Harvard University discovered, for example, that if one worker at a small firm stops smoking, his or her colleagues have a 34 percent chance of quitting. Moreover, a person in a social network is 20 percent more likely to quit smoking if someone else in that network quits, even if the two don't know each other that well.[17]

On the nonwork side, these researchers also found that a person's risk for obesity increases 37 percent if their spouse is obese, 40 percent if a sibling is obese, and 57 percent if a close friend is obese. Clearly, one's social circle both at work and at home has a profound influence on reinforcing his or her healthy or unhealthy behaviors.

Support from the managers and the resources of the organization are just as crucial to create a sustained culture of health.[18] Both incentives and consequences are important, as we've already said. But just as significant is the ability for employees to see that those in top leadership positions are also on board and participating in culture change. People learn by observing and modeling behaviors enacted by others. This is referred to as "social learning."[19] The social learning that takes place by watching others who hold power and influence over us is a powerful motivator and reinforcer.

Now that you have a better understanding of what is involved in culture change in general, it is now time to put into place a process with your employees to create a culture of health in your organization. The sample solution we offer is, again, just a sample. You intimately know your organization and its people, and you will likely want to modify these steps to fit your particular situation.

Sample Solution #3: Changing the Organizational Culture from "Unhealthy" to "Healthy"

Consider the following approach to implementing change in your organization's health culture:

1. Recognize that you won't change everyone or, at least, not at once. Pick out a few people who you believe have some influence over others in the organization and work on bringing them on board. This will allow you to use these folks later to help recruit others to join in. The people who agree will also need to be made aware that their agreement will include some personal data sharing to build support and provide "public relations" for the culture change. You don't need a lot of these folks at first, but the ones who agree should be socially powerful in your organization.

2. Set up a few (no more than three or four) indicators for which people can improve their numbers. These could be cholesterol, blood pressure, or weight. Concrete and objective goals and data tend to attract people more than vague, subjective aspirations. They are also easier for you to incent and reward.

3. Provide the facts and information to the participants. Whether an outside health care person does it or not, start with realistic data and what those data signify about health in your organization. This is the beginning of creating the shared understanding and values we talked about earlier.

4. Ask the "influential people" from Step 1 to voluntarily share their numbers publically. If they will, make a chart that shows where they are at the beginning, and then post

measurement of the chosen data monthly. Even if they won't reveal their numbers, at least publicizing that these people are involved will help others recognize the importance of participation.

5. Provide some educational opportunities (for example, "lunch and learn" sessions) so that people start learning *how* to change their behaviors. These should include behavioral and emotional techniques that are demonstrated and practiced. Encourage people to find "accountability partners" who can support each other and provide motivation and encouragement to each other. This isn't required, but given what we know about social support, it works for a lot of people! Remember that people will need time to develop new approaches and behaviors. Just like learning a new sport or any new skill, time is required to develop. And, of course, participants will need ongoing coaching and support. No one-time training event or educational program will substitute for ongoing coaching and support.

6. Create specialized language and symbols for your health culture. Language and symbolism are powerful reinforcers for culture change, primarily because they create a feeling of being part of an in-group. A cultural insider is fluent in the jargon of that culture, and so creating the health jargon specific to your organization will help solidify the efforts that all of you are engaged in. Remember, too, that the food, drink, and activities on your premises are also symbols about how the organization views health. It is not lost on most employees that if you say you are creating a healthy culture, but you still have soda and junk food machines on your premises, you aren't really serious about changing. Likewise, expecting people to stay seated in cubicles with uncomfortable and ergonomically questionable chairs also sends an unhealthy message. Walk around and audit what the symbols say about health in

your organization. The key is to make sure the symbols throughout the organization send only the messages you want to send.

7. Create a challenge contest. After the influential people from Step 1 have a month or so under their belts, ask them each to recruit one other person as a challenger. In other words, much the way the television show *Iron Chef* pits an Iron Chef against a challenger, you want to create motivation for others to want to compete. This step provides a motivational environment so people will want to change their behaviors. Encourage people to cheerlead for their favorites, and celebrate the victor and the challenger.

8. Appropriately pair rewards with behaviors and achievements. Not doing so is often one of the stupidest mistakes organizations make. Employees are asked to go above and beyond their job descriptions or to make great personal sacrifices to help out in times of need or great turmoil. Afterward, the organization rewards them with . . . a $25 gift card to a local restaurant. Really? Seriously? That's it? As a result, employees are less likely to volunteer to be a good organizational citizen the next time. Remember it isn't about the reward itself; it's about *what the reward represents* in terms of how valuable employees believe the organization and its managers think they are. So, as you consider what incentives and rewards to use, here are a few tips:

   • Start small and work up to larger rewards. If you start too high, there is nowhere to go later on. One of the worst aspects is reward plateauing, so that behaving or achieving consistently is not rewarded differently than people who do something for a short time. Remember you are after long-term change, not short-term achievement.

   • Reward behaviors as well as achievements. I may not have lost my 25 pounds, but the fact that I've stuck with walking 15 minutes a day for a month is a celebratory event!

- Realize that the reward or incentive you provide is not the reason the person is getting healthier; rather, it is a *symbol* of changing an unhealthy culture to a healthy one. Therefore, choose rewards for their symbolic effect. For example, if I have managed to walk 15 minutes every day for 6 months, a symbolic reward might be a new pair of good walking or running shoes. Every time I put them on I'm reminded of how the organization values what I'm doing.

9. Engage your health care provider in the process. There is nothing better than having your insurance provider partner with you to create your healthy culture. Many companies have resources and strategies that you can use. And, don't forget that you want them to track your utilization and cost data so that you can provide tangible results for your management team. The better the results (particularly financial ones), the more likely top management will continue to provide resources and support to sustain your healthy culture efforts.

What Do I Do Now?

The bottom line for our third common business problem—adapting to changing laws and regulations—is that an organization must first understand how the law or regulation will *factually* affect its business before it can take steps to adapt to it. This does not mean knee-jerk reactions based on rumors, unfounded fears, or media hype. Rather, it means identifying the appropriate indicators that are driving, and are being driven by, the change. In our example throughout this chapter we used health care, but it could be any legal or regulatory change. Remember: The law or regulation itself is not the problem; the problem is in how an organization adapts to it. Therefore, as you face continual changes in the laws and regulations that affect your organization, your job is to work on the following tasks:

1. Identify the reasons the law or regulation exists. In other words, what is the real underlying reason it was enacted? This will help you identify how it will likely affect your business model. For example, the PPACA was enacted primarily to make sure all Americans have affordable health insurance. Therefore, the effect on your organization is driven by whether your current employees have access to health insurance, provided either by you or by another entity.

2. Take time to understand what the law or regulation actually says and whether your organization (as it currently exists) will in fact benefit or suffer as a result. Not all laws and regulations affect organizations the same way, and there are occasions when they are helpful, not harmful! Try not to listen to all the doomsayers; rather, focus on the effects for *your* organization, and don't assume that how the law or regulation might affect others will be how it will affect you.

3. Study the fine print. Most legislation has a lot of confusing language, including special-interest issues embedded in it that don't even apply to your organization. Identify the specific issues that *will* affect you and write them in clear, understandable language. For example, "Organizations will be required to pay at least 60 percent of the health insurance premiums for any full-time employee (30 or more hours)." Then, interpret what the law or regulation will mean for your organization: "We already do this for employees who work at least 40 hours in a pay period. Our 35 part-time employees who work between 30 and 39 hours in a pay period are now required to be covered." In reality, only the first 144 pages of the PPACA apply

to employers. Of course, if your organization is a medical provider, you have a lot more pages to read!

4. Analyze the effect of the law or regulation on the organization. This means more than just the financial effects, although those are of obvious concern. But you also want to know the effect on the ability to attract and retain talent, on the organization's reputation and brand with both customers and employees, and, as we have been saying all along, on the extent to which the organization-environment fit will be able to be brought into closer alignment. That is to say, you want to know how difficult it will be for your organization to adapt to the law or regulation. This last part will require the identification of the leading and lagging indicators that will alert you to whether and how well your chosen method of responding to the change is working.

As a leader in your organization, you will become invaluable if you can do these things *and* can propose approaches and programs that will respond positively to the change in laws or regulations that affect your business. As we note throughout this book, engaging the employees in those efforts will reap long-term benefits and, ultimately, will result in a healthier, more productive, and more committed workforce.

Common Business Problem #4: Extreme Makeover: How Do We Attract and Retain the Most Competent Talent?

"Competence, like truth, beauty, and contact lenses, is in the eye of the beholder."

—*Laurence J. Peter, author of* The Peter Principle

Even though we asked in our survey that respondents avoid discussing specific HR challenges and focus, instead, on the larger organization-wide problems that keep their CEOs and directors up at night, overwhelmingly respondents mentioned "attracting and retaining the most competent employees" as one of their top headaches. We were not surprised. Invariably, as we talk to business leaders and HR professionals, the 21st century is heralding a low point in terms of finding and keeping people who possess the skills, knowledge, and competencies that organizations in all industries will need, now and in the future.

Why is that? What's going on?

We believe there are several reasons for the problem, but we begin our discussion with the idea that the organization-environment fit (in this case, the demand for workers, compared with the supply of workers with the skills required to do the jobs that are in demand) is slowly eroding.

The Changing Employment Landscape

The Fit between Organizational Labor Demand and Environmental Labor Supply Demand

The Bureau of Labor Statistics (BLS) has reported 10-year employment projections (2010-2020) for service occupations, professional occupations, and production/manufacturing occupations. According to these projections, the number of jobs in the service occupation sector (for example, health care operations, personal care, building and grounds maintenance, food preparation, protection and security) and the professional occupation sector (for example, computer science, engineering, architecture, social work, education, nursing, legal) will increase, on average, more than 30 percent by 2020.[1] Most of the service sector jobs are not particularly highly paid and do not require advanced degrees, whereas the professional occupations require at least a bachelor's degree, and many require advanced master's degrees or even doctoral degrees. As such, most of these professional jobs are also associated with higher pay than the service occupation jobs.

Conversely, certain production and manufacturing occupations (such as assemblers, metal and plastics fabricators, printers, and painters) are projected to decrease, on average, by about 15 percent at the end of 2020. Most of these jobs are traditionally associated with vocational and technical training and apprenticeships, and their average pay falls somewhere between the service and professional sectors pay levels.

Here are some more interesting facts from the BLS that may (or may not) surprise you:[2]

- Over the 2010-2020 decade, 54.8 million job openings are expected. More than half of them (61.6 percent) will come from the need to replace workers who retire or permanently leave an occupation.
- In four out of five occupations across industry sectors, the openings due to replacement needs far exceed the num-

ber that will be due to growth, including those occupations that are in decline.

- Occupations classified as needing master's degrees are projected to grow by 21.7 percent, followed by those requiring doctoral or professional degrees (19.9 percent) and associate degrees (18 percent).

- More than two-thirds of the 30 occupations expected to have the largest number of job openings will not need *any* postsecondary education or related work experience at all; rather they will require short-term, on-the-job training.

Judging from the projected demand, most of you will need a lot of replacement workers, some of whom need to be professionally trained, but most of whom will need little education or training as they enter your organization.

Are you surprised by this information? Or do these projections mirror what is going on now in your organization? Our guess is that they are starting to look that way, but you probably haven't experienced the eye of that storm yet.

Supply

The projections from a recent BLS report on the supply of workers paint an equally dire picture for many organizations. Again, here are a few basic facts from the report:[3]

- Population growth is slowing, and that also leads to slower labor force growth during the period from 2010-2020. It doesn't mean an absence of growth, though. The BLS predicts a small labor force increase of 10.5 million (about 0.7 percent) by 2020. However, this growth will likely come primarily from immigrants to our shores and retirees returning to the labor force in search of another job or even a post-retirement career change, not from the supply that most organizations have traditionally counted on (recent high school or postsecondary graduates).

- The Baby Boom generation (those born between 1945 and 1964) moves entirely into the 55-or-older age group by 2020, making its share of the labor force about 25 percent. The Generation X and Generation Y groups (ages 25-54) will drop to 63.7 percent of the labor force, and the 16- to 24-year-old age group during that period is projected to account for only 11.2 percent.
- Diversity in the labor force will also increase by 2020, with almost one-third of the available workers coming from a different racial or ethnic group than Caucasian (Hispanics—18.6 percent, Asians—5.7 percent, and Blacks—12 percent).

In addition, the International Center for Peace and Development website reports the following alarming information related to the global work supply:[4]

- The United States is forecast to have a shortage of 17 million working-age people by 2020. For example, there is already a shortfall of 126,000 nurses, and estimates indicate a shortage of 200,000 physicians and 400,000 nurses by 2020.
- China will have a deficit of 10 million workers by 2020. India will have a surplus of 47 million workers during that same time; however, this surplus will generally be low-skilled and poorly educated.
- A World Bank study estimates that 68 million immigrants will be needed to meet labor requirements in the European Union alone during the period from 2003 to 2050.[5]

What does this mean for your organization in the future? First and foremost, it means that there will be fewer available workers overall. This may not be a bad thing, given the likelihood that productivity and advancement in technology will combine to require fewer workers than you have or need right now. However, the primary problem comes in the form of a growing mismatch between the skills and locations of the available workforce (supply) and those needed by U.S. organizations (demand). Numerous research studies confirm the existence of a substantial shortage of workers with the required level of skills to fill vacant positions.[6] There are several reasons for this, but let's look at just one: how people are prepared for the workplace of tomorrow.

Preparation

A large part of the misfit between workers and jobs is that we have not kept up with preparing employees not only for the skills needed for the future, but for also basic skills expected from any high school or college graduate today. Unfortunately, the cost of workers who are unprepared and unqualified is being shouldered by U.S. businesses, which are spending more than $60 billion a year on training in basic skills, including reading, writing, and mathematics,[7] never mind higher-order skills, knowledge, and competencies. A lack of preparation for the jobs of tomorrow will not only mean a lack of access to higher-paying jobs for workers, but it also means that our nation will not be as equipped to compete in the global economy, as this quotation from the National Academy of Sciences so aptly states:

> Civilization is on the brink of a new industrial order. The big winners in the increasingly fierce global scramble for supremacy will not be those who simply make commodities faster and cheaper than the competition. They will be those who develop talent, techniques, and tools so advanced that there is no competition.[8]

Skills, Competencies, and Personal Attributes for a New Age

So what types of talent are needed? In 1991, the Secretary's Commission on Achieving Necessary Skills (SCANS) of the U.S. Department of Labor examined the implications of a rapidly changing economy and labor market on education.[9] Though this study may seem past its prime, we assure you that it is not an outdated perspective and may be even increasing in relevance.

SCANS identified five core competencies and a three-part foundation of skills and personal attributes that, combined, are necessary for success in the current and future workplace:

1. Resource management—time and money management, as well as the ability to allocate materials, space, and staff.
2. Interpersonal skills—the ability to work on teams, teach others, serve customers, take the lead, negotiate, and work with people from culturally diverse backgrounds.
3. Information management—the ability to acquire and evaluate data, organize and maintain files, interpret and communicate data, and use technology to process information.
4. Systems thinking—the ability to understand social, organizational, and technological systems, monitor and correct performance, and design or improve systems.
5. Technology use and management—the ability to select appropriate equipment or tools, use technology for specific tasks, and maintain technological equipment.

Underlying these five competencies is a core set of skills and personal attributes that workers must possess:

1. Basic skills—reading, writing, arithmetic, mathematics, listening, and speaking.
2. Thinking skills—creative thinking, decision-making, problem-solving, knowing how to learn, and reasoning from cause to effect.
3. Personal qualities—responsibility, self-esteem, sociability, self-management, and integrity.

Although it is clear that workers will need a full range of basic, thinking, and personal skill sets to be successful, employers seem to be most concerned with the lack of thinking skills and personal qualities. One survey found that the five skills most valued by the nation's largest employers are professionalism, teamwork, oral communication, ethics, social responsibility, and reading comprehension, with higher-order thinking skills and personal qualities expected to increase in importance for both high school and college graduates.[10]

You have no doubt begun to feel some of this pressure where you work. As college professors we also see the misfit between the basic and personal skill sets that students bring to college and those sought by employers. It is a real and growing problem for all organizations. But the good news is, if your organization will start responding to this problem now, there will be less scurrying at the last minute to attract and retain the talent you need.

"Pay Me Now or Pay Me Later"

The reality is that your organization has two responses to the "talent war," both of which will cost money and require an investment in time. However, the first choice will be dictated by others, whereas the second choice will let you decide how, when, and where to invest your resources. Let's look at both responses.

Response #1: Tactical Hiring and Retention

A tactic is an isolated action that takes advantage of opportunities, given a particular moment in time. In other words, a tactical approach to talent management sees a gap or a crack in the organization's talent pool and implements a specific means to fill it. By and large, this is the traditional approach to recruitment and hiring that many of you are doing now in your organizations.

It generally goes something like this: Someone in your organization sends you a personnel requisition form to fill a vacancy (or, in smaller organizations, knocks on your door and tells you, "Jane in Accounting just quit, and we need to replace her ASAP"). Then, you employ a "tactic" or means to do just that: advertising in the newspaper, posting the job on your intranet or on an Internet job board, or asking current employees, friends, or staffing firms to refer applicants to you. You may also keep records on how long it takes you to fill openings and on your turnover rates in general or in specific jobs, and the truly savvy among you may be keeping track of your recruitment yield—that is, the ratio of applicants-to-interviews and the ratio of interviews-to-hires attributable to specific recruitment sources. You may even be keeping track of how much money is spent on sourcing applicants, the amount of time spent on interviewing, and the ratio of replacement hiring to new job hiring. All of these provide useful information so that you can amend the tactics as you continue filling gaps in your talent.

As you tend to the employment needs of your organization, however, you are likely finding it difficult to locate and hire the right people at the time you need them. At least, that is what our survey respondents said were keeping them up at night. And it isn't for the lack of trying. On any given day there are countless seminars, workshops, and webinars that are all designed for you to learn the tricks to sourcing applicants.

The problem with using a tactical approach is that you are at the mercy of who is available at the time you need them and, ultimately, you are relying on others to define your talent pool, rather than creating it yourself. For example, every year a retail establishment became frustrated trying to hire team leaders to manage its kiosks at the mall during the holiday season. Even though the need to hire people occurred every year, the organization continued to wait until the end of October to begin looking for kiosk managers, and every year, it tried to find college students to fill these positions. However, every year, the company never found enough qualified people because the college students were still in school and couldn't start until too late in the shopping season. The employer ended up contracting with Labor Ready, a provider of temporary employees, to help fill its employment gaps. However, most of the employees provided were not qualified in sales, much less in management. Consequently, most of those hired were not successful at the jobs they were hired to do. Clearly, the retail organization was at the mercy of the available labor pool, no matter how unqualified, by committing the same tactical mistake year after year.

If you approach talent management in a tactical way, it is inevitable that, eventually, you will not be able to find potential, qualified employees you can attract to your organization. Merely relying on competitive salaries, employee benefits and incentives, employment branding, and other traditional lures will not attract the skilled, competent workforce for the next decade and beyond, primarily because those employees are not going to exist.

Interestingly, at the crux of the problem is our traditional focus on hiring for specific jobs. We fall into the trap of replacement hiring. If Jane in Accounting quit this morning, we focus our efforts on hiring Jane's replacement for the job she held. And although we may look at the job description and craft our recruitment and selection efforts to make sure that Jane's replacement has the skills and knowledge to do the job, we often do not consider the broader implications of hiring for just that job. This will come back to haunt organizations in the future, we assure you. Instead, organizations need to begin attracting and retaining employees (what we'll call here "human capital investment") from something other than a job-centric perspective. Let's take a look at three problems that your organization likely faces in continuing a job-centric approach, and then we'll propose some strategies for how to resolve them using human capital investment thinking.

The Problem of Job Descriptions

On the advice of most HR professionals, organizations have at least some form of job descriptions. Usually these include a job title and a brief description of the particular job, and most provide sections on the duties and responsibilities required of the job incumbent, as well as the knowledge, skills, and abilities deemed necessary to perform the job successfully. We teach this, and organizations do it; some do it better than others.

As a result, the traditional approaches to recruitment, selection, compensation, performance management, and other HR functions rely heavily on what we have come to believe is the cornerstone of human resources: a well-written, clearly-defined, detailed job description.

So what's the problem?

One of the primary problems with job descriptions is that they are . . . well . . . descriptions of *jobs*. Therefore, the fundamental use for job descriptions is to design HR programs (for example, recruiting strategies, selection tests, compensation structures, performance appraisals) based on jobs in the organization. This is the old way of hiring employees.

Consider once more our problem of Jane the accountant. Let's assume that Jane was successfully performing her job before she quit. Perhaps she had been doing it for some time, and she had it down pat. In addition, because she had been performing it for a while, she had tailored it somewhat to her particular style, preferences, skills, and abilities. We all do that, by the way. It is part of making it "our" job. Some of the tasks and duties detailed on the job description we like better than others, and some we perform better than others. However, the job description itself does not change; rather, we change the job so that it fits us better. Moreover, this usually is a subtle change that happens over time, often without anyone really acknowledging it. We take on tasks that others don't like to do or who cannot do. We shift some tasks to others because we don't like them or to make room for other ones we inherit or get assigned. Over time, job descriptions become obsolete and outdated.

HR professionals are called on periodically to update job descriptions, and it is this task that sets the stage for future problems in attracting and retaining talent. The typical process begins by looking at the outdated description and then asking incumbents and managers to decide what needs to be added, changed, or deleted. Then, after receiving that information, the job description gets rewritten (maybe even retitling the job) so that it meshes with what others believe the job entails and requires from an incumbent. So far, so good.

In the past this was followed by advertising and sourcing applicants who matched the requirements of that job. However, in the 21st century business environment, the updated job description may require things that the potential applicants don't have or can't do. You keep trying to find that elusive person who has it all or, at least, a lot of what the job description calls for, but to no avail.

Now what?

One typical approach is to raise the salary so that you are able to attract (presumably) better-qualified applicants. This sometimes works, but it often throws your compensation system out of whack, creating feelings of inequity and, ultimately, more work and headaches for you. Unfortunately, though, not every organization can afford to increase salaries high enough for this method to really work across the board.

Another approach is to outsource the job entirely so that it becomes someone else's problem. Again, depending on the job, this can be a viable solution, particularly if that solution is cost-effective *and* the results are satisfactory. Unfortunately, neither of these approaches is a long-term solution to a problem that will continue to resurface in the future.

Focusing on specific requirements for individual jobs increases the chances that at any given time you will not find someone who meets those requirements. Given our previous discussion on the impending scarcity of workers, in general, and the changing nature of organizational demands in particular, continuing with job-centric approaches to finding talent doesn't seem to be a sustainable strategy.

The Problem of Job-Person Mismatch

When Jane leaves her accounting job without much notice, some-one has to do the tasks for which Jane was responsible. Tradition-ally, most organizations assign those tasks and duties to someone else who, at least on a temporary basis, must complete them in ad-dition to those that are already a part of his or her regular assign-ments. This approach causes a multitude of issues, not the least of which are the pace and workload stressors on those employ-ees picking up the duties. As a result, productivity goes down, felt stress and strains go up for both the incumbent and customers, and the overall climate of the workplace deteriorates.

The common response is to try to fill the job as quickly as possible so these outcomes are minimized. However, as we've al-ready said, if the applicants for Jane's job are not skilled enough, we typically respond by (a) hiring them anyway, (b) reducing or amending the requirements for the job, or (c) adjusting our expec-tations downward for their performance. None of these, of course, is what we want. The problem with these responses is that as the supply of people who have the specific knowledge, skills, and abilities required by the job decreases, we end up with a job-person mismatch.

The outdated hiring approach generally responds by adjust-ing the job, not the person in the job. We shift responsibilities from the underskilled person to someone who does have the skills and competencies, thereby punishing the more competent worker by giving him or her more tasks and a greater workload (usu-ally without an accompanying increase in pay or other benefits). Sometimes we resort to "dumbing down" the job so that the less skilled employee can do it. And, occasionally, we eliminate the job altogether and go through what organizations typically refer to as "restructuring," which is basically redistributing the tasks around the organization or outsourcing them to another individual or organization.

Consider this example from an actual organization. Sylvia (not her real name) was the office administrator in a small not-for-profit organization. When she was hired she had an undergraduate degree in graphic design and some basic computer and office skills. Her job description required her to be responsible for all office tasks (for example, copying, greeting visitors, posting changes to a database, handling vendors, coordinating the organization's calendar).

At the time she was hired the organization sent out a monthly newsletter to its supporters and members through snail mail, and the task of creating the newsletter was done by one of the other staff members. Sylvia, by virtue of her interest and degree in graphic design, decided that she would like to incorporate that task into her job. She took great pride in her artistic layouts, but her English skills (grammar, spelling, writing, and editing) were not good. Soon, the executive director began to get complaints about all the errors in the newsletter and took the step of removing some of her other job duties (database and vendors) so that she would have more time to work on the newsletter. Needless to say, the errors continued.

What was wrong with this approach? Primarily, Sylvia was underskilled for the task (newsletter creation), yet her boss gave her more time to concentrate on those things she wasn't likely to get any better at (language skills) and cut out those duties that she actually was good at (managing the database and dealing with vendors). To make matters worse, the database and vendor responsibilities that Sylvia used to do well were given to someone who had no experience in doing either one and who, subsequently, was let go a few months later for performance issues. Overall, the organization tried to both (a) shift the job requirements and (b) reduce the job requirements, thereby resulting in poor performance from not just one person, but from two different people across multiple tasks.

The Problem of Person-Organization Mismatch

Often the fit problem is not with the person and the job, but with the person and the organization itself. This is usually a problem of cultural fit in that the employee doesn't accept or adapt to the values, norms, rules, symbols, or people in the particular organization. In other words, the person may be skilled at the job he or she was hired to do, but is not able to fit in with how the organization and its employees operate on a daily basis. Interestingly, the mismatch between the person and the organization is usually a prime reason for retention problems in organizations.

Some managers try to remedy this situation by requiring employees to go through "team training." They mistakenly believe that if only their people would learn how to work as a team, the attitudes and behaviors—and thus, the performance—of the employees would improve. However, the fallacy in this thinking lies in the fact that the culture of an organization is so embedded in everything (for example, systems, symbols, and values) that merely addressing interpersonal relationships and attitudes will do little to change a strong culture.

There are two real extremes in the problem of person-organization mismatch. First, if an organization attempts to hire only people who fit the culture of the firm, it will inevitably attract and retain only those people who are like the ones already there. The danger here is one of homogeneity: no new and different people, no new and different ideas. The second danger, by contrast, is one of diversity: If you have too many different types of people, the culture disintegrates, thereby causing fragmentation and increased uncertainty for both long-time employees and newer ones. Both extremes are real problems in addressing the issues of attracting and retaining talent.

Whether your organization sees homogeneity or diversity as the bigger problem, the reality is that there is a tendency to lean too far in either direction when faced with attraction and retention problems. In reality, the overarching problem is that the organization often doesn't know its own culture well enough to determine which parts of it require homogeneity and which parts need more diversity.

A local bank was notorious for experiencing high turnover in its teller ranks. This was concerning because these folks were the "face" of the bank. Customers built relationships with their tellers and were disappointed when a familiar face was gone, as evidenced by the results from customer surveys. Branch managers were asked how they might reduce teller turnover. One manager knew that the last three people who left her bank did so because they were not getting promoted when a desk job came open. They were passed over, purportedly because they didn't know the bank's products well enough to sell them. In fact, as soon as a customer showed interest, the tellers were instructed to refer them to a desk person.

Unfortunately for the banking customers, desk people were always hired from the outside, and they were usually not familiar with the local area. Therefore, they didn't know any of the customers, their families, or the local culture. Customers would get transferred to a desk person who didn't really understand them or their needs. As a result, the bank lost several sales, and, even more troubling, several customers ended up taking their business elsewhere after poor experiences with a desk person. One manager, however, had a different approach. She hired only from the local area for the majority of her openings because these local people knew their customers. They shopped at the same stores, they went to the same churches, and their children attended the same schools. In this case, understanding the culture of the town and the bank allowed the manager to recognize the importance of similarity in retaining employees and customers.

As you can see from all three problems described, organizations cannot continue to operate with outmoded approaches to attracting and retaining competent employees. What is needed are strategies that look at hiring and investing in the whole person so that, whatever occurs in our work environments, our organizations have the ability to quickly adapt. Our main point is that hiring for a particular job is the traditional approach to staffing management, while hiring for particular *skills, abilities, and competencies* is a much more effective, strategic approach.

Response #2: Strategic Human Capital Investments

Environments have changed (and will continue to change) from the last century when the future was relatively stable. Previously, human resources was expected to hire, train, and develop employees to prepare for a "predictable" upcoming business environment. Unfortunately, in a world of continuous uncertainty, using this traditional approach results in hiring, training, and developing for business and talent scenarios that may never occur. To put it another way, investing in human capital that an organization may never need can be an expensive proposition, especially if (a) you aren't sure which skills and talents you will need in the future, and (b) the employees you will need aren't talent-ready when you need them. Therefore, in consultation with top management, we must prepare for a future that can't be predicted.

Sound like an impossible task?

Primarily, if one cannot predict the future with any accuracy, then it requires preparing for a multitude of futures. By this we don't mean hiring every talent combination possible. Rather, the strategic approach means that you go after talent that has unique characteristics that are required in every organization, no matter what the future holds:

- Learning agility (also known as "trainability," it is the ability to learn a variety of new skills and knowledge when employees need to learn them).
- An adaptability and interest in working in unpredictable environments.
- Self-motivation and self-discipline.

- An ability to identify and effectively handle previously unknown problems.

Recall that one of the persistent issues for the future is preparation of employees. Historically, organizations have relied on educational institutions, apprenticeship programs, and other external means to get people ready to work in specific jobs and industries. As we move forward, these will not be sufficient to ensure that your organization will have enough talent with the right skills, abilities, and competencies when you need them. Therefore, it becomes important for you to invest in developing the talent you will need yourselves.

What Is Talent?

To begin the process of human capital investment, an organization must first change how it views talent. One interesting note is that there seems to be no commonly agreed-on meaning for "talent."[11] Generally, talented employees are considered to be the high-worth, hard-to-find-and-keep people. As such, this definition of talent considers both the organization's demand for valued employees (which would be those who, by virtue of their skills, abilities, and competencies, add value to the organization and, thus, to its customers or clients) and the labor market supply of people who possess those valued skills, abilities, and competencies. It sometimes becomes a puzzle to figure out an organization's talent mix (see Figure 6.1).

If we look at talent in this way, we can see that there are four types of employees employed by organizations.[12] From this perspective, if we consider the future problem of the increasing demand and eroding supply of "difficult to replace" workers discussed earlier, we can also see that some will be of high value and some will be of low value.

But what does this really mean?

In the current environment it means that employees who do not add much value to an organization and are also difficult to replace will probably see their jobs outsourced in the future. Unfortunately, some HR professionals may fall victim to this perception (which is why we are writing this book so that they are seen as adding real value to organizations), as well as some lower- and middle-level managers.

For those employees who are easy to replace and don't add a lot of value, technology will replace some of these people and already has. Think about bank tellers and how they are continually being replaced by ATM machines and online banking. Many other service workers and production employees will also likely be replaced by advances in technology. Have you driven through a toll booth lately? Not only are there automated ticket dispens-

Figure 6.1 The Replacement Value Puzzle

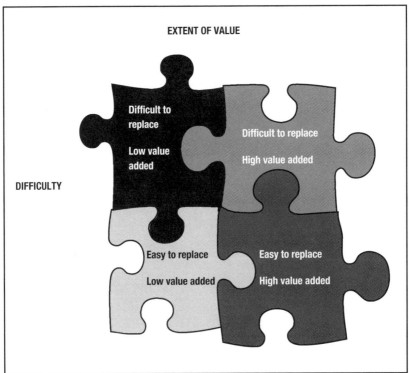

ers when you enter the turnpike, but many now have self-service payment or E-ZPass lanes at the exits instead of an actual person.

Looking at talent this way may still be seen as an organization's reactive response to its environment and not a proactive, strategic decision. Though this response is inevitable sometimes, it is one of proportion. Current thinking is that the low-value workers need more training so that they will provide higher value. But this gets us right back to our initial problem: preparation. If we argue that external educational and training sources will not provide enough high-value, competent employees in the future, where are they to come from?

Employees who are easy to replace and who add value to your organization will be in high demand across organizations, which is why you must act now to hire them and work on retaining them. Currently, for example, it is fairly easy to find people who are available to work in customer service. This particular occupation doesn't usually require post-high school education or extensive work experience (although some organizations are starting to reconsider educational requirements for these types of positions). So you may have a lot of candidates who are "blank slates" that can be trained and honed to your organization's requirements. Really talented customer service employees create a great deal of value for your customers and, ultimately, for your organization. The problem is finding available people who are also good at customer service. A crucial step is acting now to develop those skills within your current workforce and, additionally, to hire for the potential development of those employees.

Finding the people who are difficult to replace, but create a ton of value for your company, requires a different strategy. Those employees, whose supply is limited, are likely difficult to replace because they possess skills and competencies already in high demand. Therefore, your job is to increase your own supply.

One example of this is in the medical profession. It is widely known that the supply of nurses and doctors is shrinking, and, of course, the preparation time for doctors is especially long. One hospital that we know of has a long-term strategy to help it supply doctors and nurses to its more rural hospitals and clinics. It begins by cultivating interest in medicine with kids in middle schools and high schools located in the rural areas the hospital serves. Its premise is that people trained in large cities tend to stay in large cities, both because of inertia and because of the amenities larger cities have. But, the hospital administrators reason, people who grew up in rural areas are more likely to want to stay or return there to raise families; therefore, providing a guarantee of a job might be a powerful motivator. So, the hospital provides mentoring, participation in science events, and scholarships to students from those towns who express an interest in medicine. Although it is too soon to tell if this strategy will pay off in the next generation, it is certainly a novel and strategic approach to developing the talent the hospital will need in providing health care to residents in smaller towns and rural areas.

Another illustration of this type of tactic is hospitals that offer to pay off student loans for doctors and nurses if they agree to stay with the hospital for an extended period of time (usually 10 years). Such loan repayment plans are more common in less desirable locations, such as certain rural or inner city areas that have difficulty attracting medical professionals.

Everybody Has Talent

As you can see, the problem of attracting and retaining competent talent is not going away anytime soon. Therefore, we would like for you to consider a completely different view: All employees, at all levels in your organization, should be considered to have talent and encouraged to maximize their respective potential. From a strategic point of view, the benefit of seeing employees this way opens up the possibility that attracting and retaining talent may provide your organization with a competitive advantage. Creating a talent-full organization provides a valuable resource that is not able to be imitated or duplicated by competitors. Let's talk about how that might be done.

Moving away from a Focus on Jobs

In today's organizations, the focus should be on hiring for competencies like learning agility, adaptability, problem-solving, and several more, as we mentioned earlier, rather than for job-specific knowledge and skills. Moving away from a focus on hiring for specific jobs and moving toward a focus on hiring for employee development basically solves the three problems (that is, job descriptions, job-person mismatch, and person-organization mismatch), because it shifts an organization's reliance from others creating an available talent pool to one that is created specifically for the organization's own future needs. To do that means that the organization must decide now what those competencies and abilities are and, further, where they will be needed in the organization.

This view further implies that all talent should *not* be treated similarly. Rather, in any organization, there will be places for which small increments in talent improvement will yield large returns and, therefore, will have a critical impact on what the organization is trying to do. Conversely, other employees may be desirable to retain, but their development may not generate additional significant results. These are decisions you will need to make based on your own distinct situation. Every organization is different, with different talent requirements and configurations.

Consider this situation from our previous banking example. There was a teller who was a high-potential employee for whom the manager decided to take a leap of faith. Although the teller had great relationships with her customers, she was not familiar enough with the products. Instead of watching her leave like so many tellers before her, the manager decided to train her on the products and how to sell them. The manager created a hybrid role in which the teller maintained her regular position for 20 hours each week, but then spent the other 20 hours learning the products. When a customer wanted to hear more about a product the teller offered, instead of just referring him or her to a desk person, the teller would walk with the customer to the desk person, and then actually sit with the customer and learn about the product as well. After a few lessons the teller began to lead the conversations while the desk person observed and was available to help out as necessary. It was not an intimidating environment at all, and when the next desk job opened, the teller was promoted into it. She knew the products, and she knew the customers. It was a win-win and set the stage for having bench strength at the branch; turnover soon became a non-issue as more tellers wanted to be trained on the financial products offered by the bank.

Moving toward a Focus on Competencies

One of the first tasks to begin a focus on competencies rather than on jobs is to have a serious discussion with the management in your organization. The purpose for the discussion is to discover what the organization values in its employees and which competencies are required to demonstrate those values. Let's take just one example from our earlier discussion on learning agility.

What do we mean, specifically, by "learning agility"? Obviously, it means that a person is able to be trained, but that doesn't really tell us what is involved in that ability. Here are three aspects to consider.

One aspect has to do with how quickly a person grasps the idea and content you are trying to teach. You may have hired someone who needed things explained or demonstrated over and over again before "getting" it, although once the employee did, he or she was fine. But hiring people who catch on quickly will save all of us time and energy.

A second indicator is perseverance and dependability, that is, employees who always follow through on their commitments, are always true to their word, and always complete their assignments on time. A person like this is likely not only to be an ideal employee but an ideal trainee as well, because not every skill or behavior is easily learned and demonstrated. When an employee sticks with learning and can be counted on to keep trying, we are more likely to want to invest the time and money in his or her training and development.

A third aspect of learning agility is open-mindedness. This is critical, because closed-minded employees tend to resist any idea or approach that may be different from their own. Additionally, they are often in denial about problems, don't see their part in creating problems, and are more likely to blame others for problems. If you are interested in having employees and managers who are able to identify and work with others on previously unknown problems, then open-mindedness is a basic requirement for learning agility.

There may be several more indicators of whether someone has learning agility. However, the beauty of learning agility is that it is applicable across the organization, whether the focus is on entry-level employees or high-level managers. When we focus on competencies like learning agility, we are able to create employees who get excited about development, are more motivated to learn new competencies, and ultimately, are more likely to want to remain with our organizations because of the investments we are willing to make in them.

Avoiding Person-Job Mismatch

As we mentioned previously, the traditional approach of trying to find a person with some exact job requirement often results in changing the job to fit the person you can find. An approach focused on competencies, on the other hand, looks at a job differently. Here a job is viewed as being made up of several tasks that, when combined, form a set of competencies and behaviors that can be trained and developed separately. The implication of this view is that several people in the organization may be able to acquire these competencies. The great part about this is that training and development in your organization can be more efficient and effective when it is focused more specifically on a specific set of competencies, and it allows for practically anyone in the organization to participate. As a result, rather than searching for one person who can do everything, you have a lot of people who can do multiple things.

The focus on competency also plays into an organization's desire to have strong bench strength in multiple areas. For example, many of you may work for organizations that have decided they need to begin succession planning. Identifying high-potential employees is often seen as inequitable and becomes demotivating for those employees not chosen to participate. By focusing on competency development you avoid these feelings and perceptions. Though not everyone will be able to develop every competency, you will gain a lot more participation across the board as increasing numbers of employees realize that they can improve their skills over time. The ultimate result is more competent employees overall who can be tapped from across the organization to serve in a variety of roles. Not only is this good for the organization in filling hard-to-replace positions, but it is also motivating for employees to learn new skills and behaviors.

Avoiding Person-Organization Mismatch

A focus on competencies also allows us to identify areas in our organizations where similarity in thinking and behaving is important, as well as those areas in which diversity may be even more important. To demonstrate what we mean, let's consider two separate areas: accounting and marketing.

It is highly likely that an accountant needs to hold similar views, values, and ethical orientation as the other accountants in the organization. Otherwise, judgment about how financial resources are used and reported could be wildly different across the accounting department. Because such judgment could have both legal and financial ramifications, we want all our accountants to be on the same page when it comes to tending our books and providing us with financial information to use in our decision-making.

On the other hand, it is equally likely that we might like a bit more diversity of thinking and multiple approaches to problem-solving in our marketing or advertising departments. How a product is to be marketed and sold requires creativity; we don't want all the people employed in marketing or advertising to see only one way of doing things.

When we hire someone who has demonstrated creativity, we are not likely to put him or her into the accounting department, given that that culture rewards both uniformity of thinking and behaving, as well as following strict rules and laws. Rather, we are likely to consider creativity more in line with a marketing or advertising culture, and therefore, the person's competency will be rewarded in those areas, making a much better person-organization fit experience.

Now it's time to provide a sample solution to help you begin the process of developing your own supply of competent, skilled employees. As always, you will need to modify these steps to fit your particular situation. The basic process, however, should work no matter which competency or competencies you choose.

Sample Solution #4: Identifying and Developing Competencies

The sample approach we present here assumes that you have had several conversations with the top and middle managers in your organization about the values and strategic direction your organization intends to promote. The buy-in for this is imperative; without it, you won't be able to accomplish much of anything related to competency development. It might even be worth your while to present managers with the statistics with which we began this chapter so that they see the urgency in beginning now. It's hard to argue against these figures, which are based on official U.S. census data and other government reports compiled from information reported by real organizations and people!

Step 1: Identifying Required Organizational Competencies

Once you have buy-in to begin this process, you first need to get a sense of the overall set of organizational competencies needed to successfully operate in your company. These competencies should be broad ones—things we mentioned earlier, like learning agility, problem-solving, communication, and so on. You don't need a million of them, just a set that reflects competencies needed to some degree in every department and job throughout your organization.

Next, you need to define what they actually mean. This is often the downfall of competency development. Much like what we did with the example of learning agility, you need to identify what precisely is involved in demonstrating the competency when it is done well and when it is done poorly. Such clarification is needed to design the selection methods to hire for these basic competencies, as well as to structure the training needed to develop them in your current employees.

Step 2: Identifying Competent Current Employees

Once you know which specific competencies you are looking for, the next step is to identify people in your organization who effectively demonstrate those competencies. This will likely require several meetings with managers in your organization to have them identify direct reports who possess the desired competencies. We also recommend asking a cross-section of employees to help prioritize the competencies. This could be done through an interview or through a brief e-mail survey.

However you wish to do it, the primary goal is to understand more fully the behaviors that represent the competencies and how employees became competent at them. This is often difficult because many people who are good at something can't tell you why they are good at it or how they became proficient.

Consider making a hard-boiled egg, for example. If you've never boiled an egg and you ask someone who does it all the time, the person will tell you, "Put the eggs in boiling water and let them cook for 15 minutes. It's simple." But actually there is more to it than that. If you really have never done it, you might wonder, "Do I turn on the burner first and put the egg in boiling water? Or, do I put the eggs in the pan with the cold water and then turn on the burner?" Then, another dilemma: "When should I start the timer: at the beginning of the cold water or after the water is boiling?" This may sound silly to you, but if you think about it, most cooks tend to do the same thing with familiar, time-tested recipes when asked how they make something. They often say, "I don't know how I make it; I don't really have a recipe; I just throw things together."

This same thing happens with employees and managers who have developed certain competencies over time. To find out how a person acquired a competency, it is necessary to understand the idea of *tacit knowledge* and to be able to structure what is called Generative Knowledge Interviewing™ (see below).

What Is Tacit Knowledge?

During the course of our lives, we acquire at least two fundamentally different types of knowledge. "Explicit knowledge" refers to the knowledge that is consciously known, that is, the specific skills, ideas, methods, and concepts that can be easily shared through speaking and writing. This knowledge is generally the focus of academic and other formal learning environments. By comparison, "tacit knowledge" refers to the vast amount of how-to knowledge people possess but are not aware of consciously. It is the unconscious insights, frames of reference, criteria, hunches, and capacities that people acquire as they learn to respond to the challenges of everyday life. Picture yourself driving a car, riding a bicycle, or using a keyboard. You know how to do those things so well that you don't actually have to know how to do them; in fact, you do them without thinking. This hidden knowledge is also gained through the automatic insights and "a-ha" moments people have as they encounter new experiences and overcome challenging problems and situations—what some people refer to as the "college of hard knocks."

Research shows that tacit knowledge, which lies beyond the realm of cognition (and, therefore, cannot be identified through mere self-reflection), is essential to the development of expertise.[13] The more someone becomes competent or expert in a given task, subject area, or role, the more likely it is that essential know-how knowledge will recede into the tacit realm.

The kinds of unconscious skills and competencies a person develops (one's tacit knowledge) are influenced by both conditions of the external environment and the innate interests, tendencies, talents, and inclinations that person already possesses. Consider a child who, at an early age, develops perfect pitch, can focus on sounds for a long period of time, and can make music from nearly anything, including instruments he or she has never played before. Having these innate capacities, though, does not mean the child will have the kinds of opportunities that are needed to develop those capabilities into the expressed competencies of a great musician.

It is generally assumed that the more a person's capacities are nurtured in a supportive environment, the more likely it is that the person will develop actual behavioral competencies. Therefore, our task as HR professionals and organizational leaders is to identify these capabilities and then provide opportunities for their development. To identify them, however, we need a structured way to discover them in the first place.

How to Conduct a Generative Knowledge Interviewing™

Because we cannot consciously identify our tacit knowledge on our own, it has to be determined via another means—in this case Generative Knowledge Interviewing™. This technique provides a means of interviewing for knowledge acquisition that, although initially designed for coaching, can be readily applied to understand the tacit knowledge underlying a person's competencies.[14] In these types of interviews, the interviewer asks the person to recount stories to uncover how the person understands and responds to specific roles and contexts. Specifically, you want to hear stories of (a) great successes, (b) significant challenges, and (c) revelatory and enlightening moments. Your goal is to hear how the person thought about and responded to the significant moments. Through skillful interviewing, you will be able to gain key insights and lessons from these stories. The authors further elaborated on their method (the direct quotation was edited slightly for our purpose):

> Specifically, the employee is asked to describe the context and sequence of her experiences in detail: things noticed, decisions made (and why), "a-ha" moments experienced, challenges faced, and so on. During this stage, the person is asked some questions, but primarily the interviewer listens. During these interviews, the interviewer engages in a form of "generative" listening intended to identify the unique patterns, themes, capacities, and so on that were embedded within the . . . stories, but not actually spoken.[15]

Once the interview is completed, the interviewer writes up an initial document that teases out and describes the tacit decisions, values, insights, and so on that comprise the employee's stories. This document is then sent to managers to review and validate with additional stories that demonstrate or refute the core competencies identified by the employees.[16] Once these are validated, the core competencies are described as fully as possible using the examples. The final document is then used to develop selection tests, to create behavioral interview questions, and ultimately, to design experiences and projects that can help employees (current and new hires) develop their expertise.

Here is an example of what we mean, beginning with a person identified as being proficient at the competency and then progressing through the process:

Example of Behavioral Competency: Learning Agility

Identifying the Tacit Knowledge through Stories

1. Describe one of your most *rewarding* learning experiences. What happened? What made it so rewarding?
2. Describe one of your most *challenging or difficult* learning experiences. What happened? How did you handle it?
3. Describe one of your most *memorable* training experiences. What happened? What made it so memorable?

Generating the Competencies Inherent in the Stories

1. Rewarding learning: Employee learned a complicated procedure for customer returns in a short period of time (30 minutes), which was practiced just an hour or so later, and she did it perfectly with no mistakes. Themes noted: rapidity of learning, immediate practice.
2. Challenging learning: Employee recounted the difficulty of learning how to generate reports from a new customer database. She found the written instructions confusing and was not able to sit down with anyone to be shown/walked through the process. Themes noted: challenge in understanding printed material, need for visual demonstration.
3. Memorable training: Employee thinks that what made her sales training memorable was that her trainer (who was also her sales manager) was able to demonstrate exactly

what he wanted, had her practice it with him multiple times, and then allowed her to actually demonstrate her skill with a customer the next day. Afterward he provided feedback on what she did right and wrong, and then made her practice it again with him. Themes noted: multiple practice sessions, immediate and specific feedback received.

Reflecting Back to the Storyteller What You Heard

Once the storyteller has recounted the example, it is helpful to clarify what you heard so that you and the storyteller are in agreement with your interpretation:

1. "You find the ability to learn something quickly and then to practice it is the most rewarding for you. Does that sound right?"
2. "You seem to be most challenged by having to read and understand printed material on your own. You prefer to learn through watching a proficient person demonstrate what you are supposed to learn. Does that seem to capture the biggest challenge of learning for you?"
3. "You remember best when you are allowed to practice the behaviors or tasks multiple times and when specific feedback is given right away on what you do well and what you don't do as well. Does that sound right to you?"

Generating the Characteristics of Learning Agility

Once you have clarified the points of the story, it is time to state the characteristics that define what is meant by the concept:

1. Learns complicated material quickly if allowed to practice it multiple times.
2. Learns best by having the material or behavior demonstrated correctly at the beginning.

3. Remembers material when immediate and specific feedback is given.

Validation of the Competencies

It is important to make sure there is agreement between the employee and the manager on the competency and the characteristics that describe it. Therefore, repeating the same process with the manager can help validate the competency and the characteristics that define it:

- The characteristics are given to each employee's manager, who gives other examples of the three questions (most rewarding, challenging, and memorable learning and training) that he or she has observed in "trainable" or "learning agile" employees.
- The same process of teasing out the characteristics is repeated with the manager's stories.
- The interviewer writes up all the information and revises the descriptions of the competency "Learning Agility," to reflect the aspects heard and interpreted though the stories and examples.

Step 3: Developing Selection Methods to Identify Competencies in Applicants

By the time you reach this step, you should be able to define and describe each specific competency and what might be involved in demonstrating proficiency in it. The final step is to determine selection methods for identifying employees who possess the competency and, later, training methods for teaching it to others.

In this example, one method that you might choose for selection is reminiscent of how you initially determined the competencies. Namely, asking behavioral interview questions is probably one of the best ways to get at the hard-to-demonstrate competencies, like learning agility.

Depending on the competency you want to assess in candidates, you may choose actual paper-and-pencil tests, work sample tests, or other methods. For example, if you wanted to hire a machine operator who had mechanical ability, you might decide to break down a machine or tool to see if he or she could put it back together without any instructions. Again, the specific competencies you want should dictate how you measure them.

Common Business Problem #5: Future Shock: How Do We Deal with a Changing Society?

"The future always comes too fast and in the wrong order."

—*Alvin Toffler, author of* Future Shock

In Alvin Toffler's classic book from 1970, he defines "future shock" as the perception of "too much change in too short a period of time."[1] We are sure that many of you reading this book would heartily agree that things are changing, often unpredictably and at a rapid pace.

Be forewarned that this fifth and final problem is somewhat of a catch-all for many of the respondents' fears about what will happen to their organizations in a society facing continual changes in social norms, technology, and leadership.

Which Changes Pose the Most Concern?

Given all of the changes facing organizations with respect to shifts in demography, increased use of and demand for technology, and changes in the needs and values for both customers and employees, it is no wonder that organizations trying to cope with some or all of these changes are also trying to decide, "Which of these should be our highest priority?"

Based on several comments from our respondents, we will begin with the issue of changing social norms and values, move from there to the challenges posed by technological advances, and finish with the ubiquitous problem of finding leaders who can deal with all of the persistent problems we've discussed in this book. Along the way these will intersect, as we are sure you are noticing in your own organizations.

The Problem of Changing Social Norms and Values

As we discussed at length in Chapter 6, demographic changes in the population's age, race, ethnicity, economic status, and geography have resulted in problems for organizations trying to find and keep talented employees. However, along with these shifts in demography have come changes in societal norms and values. Let's examine how these can have profound effects on organizations and the people who work for and buy from them.

What Are Values?

Values represent guiding principles that influence the attitudes we hold and how we choose to act. Our values are affected by a wide range of things, not the least of which are past experiences, cultural norms, and sociopolitical situations. Values have been shown to influence our political persuasions, our career choices, our ecological footprints, how much money we spend and on what, and our feelings of personal well-being.[2]

One of the interesting findings from the years of research on values is that they are *universal*.[3] First, this means that we all rely on our values to some extent to guide our behavior. Second, it means that some values are held by everyone to a degree, no matter where you live, how old you are, or what your past experiences have been. This means that customers, employees, and vendors will be looking at the values demonstrated by the organizations with which they do business and, importantly, at how well those values mesh with their own.

One a prominent researcher on the subject of values has found that there are some values (such as self-direction, hedonism, achievement, power, conformity, security, tradition, benevolence, stimulation, and universalism) that influence what people in all parts of the world think, feel, and do.[4] People hold these values with varying degrees of strength at various times in their lives, and they define them differently as they move through the world.

One's level and type of education, the media, and social pressures are likely to influence the kinds of values seen as relevant to particular situations and at particular times. As an example, you may remember after the September 11th attack that the importance of the "security" value held by most people increased dramatically, fueled in part by the media coverage of the event, but also related to one's previous experiences with people of different religious faiths and how one defined "freedom." The bottom line is that both the importance and influence of values change as our experiences change. This is the predicament in which organizations find themselves—how to keep up with these constant shifts in values.

How Experiences Shape Our Values

Throughout the years many prominent societal experiences have changed how people view the world, how those views influence the values they hold dear, and how those values shape their behaviors. For example, social movements, such as the labor movement in the early part of the 20th century and the civil rights movement in the mid-20th century, played significant roles in embedding values such as equality and social justice in policy, laws, and the wider society. One study has shown that between 1968 and 1971, the value of equality increased in importance in ranking from the seventh place to the third place among U.S. citizens, suggesting that the civil rights movement likely played an instrumental role in this change.[5] We have also seen a focus on equality more recently in the increasing attention paid to marriage equality by organizations that have begun to offer full benefits to lesbian, gay, bisexual, and transgender partners, despite relatively few states having laws that require them to do so.

Organizations seeking to adapt to a changing society must be open to shifting their social values accordingly. These societal changes signal differences in expectations among workers, customers, clients, vendors, and organizational leaders. Therefore, the values organizations respond to, the outlets they provide for expression of social values, and the policies they create will reinforce certain values and have notable effects on the attitudes and behaviors expressed by employees and customers.

As an example, some organizations have recognized the value of providing a means for employees with accumulated leave to donate that leave to another employee in need who has little leave, thereby promoting the value of being in a caring community. Such paid time off (PTO) donation programs have become popular among employees who want to contribute in some small way to co-workers who have experienced a catastrophic illness or injury and who have exhausted all of their own accrued time.

An employee at one of Sheri's former employers had barely started with the company when she was diagnosed with terminal cancer. She was not eligible for family medical leave, and she didn't yet have a week of accumulated PTO. Her daughter was getting married, and her last wish was that she'd be alive to attend the wedding. Her co-workers approached Sheri offering to donate their accrued vacation time. Sheri approached the CFO to see if that was possible, but he said no because the value of each person's PTO would be different.

Sheri created some scenarios to show how the company would actually save money if the higher-paid employees would donate their vacation time to lower-paid employees in need. The CFO thought it was too complicated, and there were no guarantees of who would donate and how they'd account for any discrepancies in pay differences for the giver and the receiver. Finally, Sheri approached the president who said he liked the leave donation idea and to work something out.

Instead of worrying about the value of each person's PTO, an hour-for-hour calculation was used, in which the leave was paid at the receiving employee's wage. In this example, the terminally ill employee was at a lower level within the organization, so using this calculation method saved the company money. The employees who were able to donate were grateful to be able to extend their co-worker's livelihood and to help her attend her daughter's wedding. The employee died shortly after the wedding, but employees who donated leave time felt they had made a real difference.

Some organizations have even extended these internal leave donation programs in response to recent tragedies, such as Hurricane Sandy. In essence, this is a "charitable" PTO donation program where employees may donate the value of their unused or unwanted PTO to a charitable organization. The employer typically pays the organization cash equal to the value of the donated PTO, which the donating employee must generally recognize as taxable compensation income subject to income tax and FICA withholding. Because the value of the PTO is donated to a charitable organization, the donor employee is then allowed a charitable contribution deduction. The employer is allowed a deduction for the value of the donation as compensation expense. In certain situations, the Internal Revenue Service (IRS) has even allowed employees to avoid recognizing the value of PTO donated to a charitable organization as compensation income.[6]

Though societal values influence organizational values, there is also a reciprocal effect: Organizational values influence society's values. Starbucks is a prime example of the positive influence of one organization on how society has changed its views and behaviors around coffee and the people who produce it and sell it. In 1995, the company developed a set of beliefs that has guided its business model ever since and, ultimately, has changed lives in coffee-producing countries. By focusing on the values of human dignity, diversity, and environmental protection, Starbucks has influenced societal perceptions of those values, ultimately making it one of the most well-regarded and frequented businesses in the world.

Unfortunately, we have also seen many instances of the reverse effect. The financial debacles over the past several years shifted society's opinion of and confidence in large financial institutions from good to poor and, in some cases, to perceptions that they are downright unethical, primarily as a result of the well-publicized scandals.[7]

Organizations must understand and adapt to changing cultural and societal values, but first they must frame their own values so that society understands what they are and what they stand for. Neither one, of course, is quick or easy.

Framing Values

Much as a picture frame imposes a boundary on what is viewed and communicated in a picture, a "values frame" imposes a boundary around what we want people to understand about those things that our organizations hold sacred. At the risk of bringing up a sensitive topic here, consider the frames in which the health care reform debate has been viewed. One side of the debate has framed health care reform as a "universal individual right," whereas the other side has framed it as "individual rights infringement." Neither one is completely right or wrong, but the facts and concerns we include in our framing of a value can make a real difference in how the message is conveyed and how it is interpreted.

So, what does this mean for your organization and how it adapts to changing values in our society?

The Problem of Fit between Social and Organizational Values

We spent some time in Chapter 3 discussing the importance of creating shared values in your organization. The basis of the challenge reported by our survey respondents really boiled down to an eroding fit between changes in social values and norms and those of their organizations. At its core, the frustration is that an organization, albeit a microcosm of society, generally lags behind society in changing its values. We believe what our respondents were characterizing is the frustration of trying to appease everybody, thereby sending mixed messages in the attempt. So, first, let's consider the mismatch between an organization's values and those of its employees, customers, clients, and the larger society— a phenomenon known as "organizational schizophrenia."

The Problem of Organizational Schizophrenia

Although the term "schizophrenia" is a category of mental disorder, some of its key characteristics also apply to organizations. Schizophrenia, in the clinical sense, implies a split between a person's thoughts and emotions. Schizophrenics display inappropriate thought patterns that often do not match the emotions they display. And although genetic predispositions to schizophrenia certainly exist, many experts have concluded that the situations people experience can also create or trigger schizophrenic responses.

One such experience is referred to as a "double bind." In essence, in a double bind situation a person receives mixed messages about appropriate behaviors or emotions and, no matter which choice is made, it becomes a no-win situation.[8] For example, if your mother gives you two sweaters—a blue one and a red one—and you wear the blue one, a double bind is created when your mother remarks, "You must not like the red one." Interestingly, in most double binds, the messages come from those in authority, and the person caught in the double bind generally has also internalized an implicit or explicit message, "Don't question authority."

Organizational schizophrenia is experienced in the contradiction of one message ("We encourage innovation, so be creative and take risks"), compared with another, competing message ("Don't make mistakes, or you'll never be successful here"). Sometimes double binds are institutionalized. A leader may tell people that he or she wants to encourage collaboration, but that message is contradicted by the reward and recognition systems in the organization that only award individual contributions. In other words, in a schizophrenic organization, "you're damned if you do and damned if you don't."

In trying to understand the role that organizational schizophrenia may play in the challenge of adapting to our changing society, let's look at how an organization might send conflicting messages in what it says it values and how it actually responds. For our first example, we'll use one that you are probably dealing with right now: work-family conflict. Organizations are dealing with a work-family value shift that is gaining in importance throughout society, and it is particularly strongest in the younger generation of workers.

We don't want to rehash everything you've probably already heard about the issue of generational differences. In some ways, the whole thing is meaningless because there is as much variation within a generation as there is between and among generations. Stereotyping notwithstanding, society is experiencing some shift in the strength and importance of universal values when it comes to the intersection of work and family. Consider this actual situation.

Greg (not his real name) was the president of a credit union. This organization opened at 8:00 a.m. and closed at 4:00 p.m. Monday through Friday. It employed five tellers, all women, who were between the ages of 19 and 35. Greg contacted Dale (who was serving in his consultant capacity) about a problem he was having with his tellers' punctuality, and he wondered what he could do to encourage them to come to work on time.

Greg's perspective was that his tellers lacked motivation and commitment. His explanation was that "you can't find people who want to work and do a good job anymore." Greg gave Dale the organization's employee manual that included, among other things, an attendance policy. Dale also interviewed three of the tellers. After reading the entire employee manual and thinking about the tellers' responses, Dale met with Greg again and explained that he saw contrary messages being sent to employees, that is, what the employee manual asserted, what the attendance policy said, and what the tellers' real situations were. For example, the manual included the following (paraphrased) statement: "[Name of credit union] believes that supporting our employees helps them attain the highest level of customer service to our members."

The attendance policy indicated that the employees would be terminated after being late to work more than three times in three months. Additionally, the tellers had explained to Dale that although they were hardly ever absent, they often got to work 10 to 15 minutes late because they had to take their children to school or to a day care, neither or which opened until 8:00 a.m. Because they were single mothers, they had no other viable option except to take their children themselves. In other words, the tellers *wanted* to be there on time, but they felt that the message of support in the manual and the message conveyed in the tardiness policy were sending mixed signals. Moreover, because they held a strong "family" value, they felt pulled in two directions—in other words, the tellers felt that they were in a double bind. Ultimately, Dale made the suggestion that the credit union open at 8:30 a.m., rather than at 8:00 a.m., which Greg promptly rejected, even though the number of customers between those two times rarely exceeded more than one or two people.

Sounds silly, doesn't it? But that is organizational schizophrenia at its best (or worst). The interesting thing is that leaders in schizophrenic organizations usually don't realize (or, sometimes, don't care) that they are sending competing, no-win messages to employees. But more toxic is that these messages also convey that the organization's values are often at odds with the society's values. In the credit union situation, the work/life concerns of the tellers are indicative of the larger society's shifting value of the fit between work and the rest of people's lives. By ignoring that value shift, Greg's decision not to adapt to that value change caused the organization's values to lag behind society's values.

Sometimes the values stated by the organization are in keeping with society's values, but they are lived out inconsistently throughout the organization, often resulting in feelings of inequity and unfairness. In our second example from a health care organization, an insurance company included among its values, "fostering a safe environment," "recognizing work/life balance," and "empowering employees." As an employee there, Sheri was required to travel two hours to the company's headquarters every other day, and then drive back home after an already exhausting 10-hour workday. In addition to mentioning the safety concerns of driving when she was tired, Sheri presented her boss with a proposal that also saved money by having the company pay for an overnight hotel stay instead of continuing to reimburse her mileage, tolls, and parking. Unfortunately, her manager said that she didn't have the cost of a hotel included in her budget, even though Sheri pointed out that the $184-per-week savings in travel would surely offset the lack of a hotel line item. She was told that the answer remained no and that she should just move closer or rent an apartment in the area.

However, her colleagues began to notice her fatigue and let her know that other directors in the company did pay for overnight accommodations. It was clear that other directors in the company understood the importance of safety and balancing work with family life; however, the particular director Sheri worked for was not "walking the talk." Sheri continued with the travel for an additional two months, at which time Sheri was the fifth person to leave that department in the boss's 10-month tenure.

What Happens to Schizophrenic Organizations?

As you can see, it is important for managers to represent their companies in ways that consistently reflect core values. Schizophrenia in organizations develops when a pattern of mixed messages occurs across multiple situations or from multiple authority figures. Over time, this leads employees to become tentative about what they say and do, to become apathetic about their jobs and organizations or, worse, to be active combatants against their leaders and companies. In essence, employees who work for schizophrenic organizations become the organization's worst nightmare. And it is no different for customers and clients of schizophrenic organizations. They can bring organizations to their knees, too.

From the organization's perspective, the tendency is to hunker down and be less likely to change when confronted with employees, customers, and clients who seemingly don't care, who are posting negative comments on social media, or who are telling their friends not to work for or buy from the organization. As a result, the organization starts down a spiral of value entrenchment, with leaders refusing to recognize the part they play in creating the problem. Moreover, by holding fast to their policies and values, even when it is clear that they don't mesh with those of their employees, their customers, or society at-large, leaders begin taking fewer risks in everything related to the organization. When an organization becomes so entrenched in its values and ways of doing things, risk aversion is the brake that keeps it from changing.

Regaining the Fit between Societal and Organizational Values

Even if your organization has started down that spiral of entrenchment, there is still hope for regaining a better fit between what society values and what the organization values. To begin, we need to identify the organization's core values (discussed in Chapter 3), which, you may remember, are those values that form the foundation by which an organization conducts its business. They are a constant reminder of what the organization really is and what it really stands for, even when the environment changes. *Even when societal values change, an organization's core values should not change.*

For example, one of the stated core values of an organization might be "respect and honor differences." We have seen increased inclusion of different people in society, either by law or by choice, and these differences are being felt in politics, education, medicine, religion, and business. Despite some organizations having increased the number of women and minorities employed, many have not changed their training or promotion criteria, their benefits plans, their committee structures, or their employment policies to be in sync with an increasing number of diverse employees. As a result, despite the fact an organization is trying to adapt to a changing society (by changing how the organization "looks"), its "respect and honor differences" value is not being implemented fully so that it fails to truly incorporate those differences in how it operates on a daily basis (by changing how the organization "feels"). Thus, the organization's value—though it seems to be in alignment with society's value—isn't. This situation often results in the leaders of the organization not being able to fathom why they are still having problems attracting and retaining women and minorities. But the *real* culprit is not a change in the value, per se, but the contradiction in how the value is interpreted by society and how it is lived out by the organization.

One way to make sure that the values of the organization are transparent to applicants might be to include interview questions that reflect organizational values (for example, "Can you recount a time in your previous job in which you were able to see someone else's difference as a strength for your organization or team?"), as well as to evaluate the performance of employees and managers on the extent to which they demonstrate the organization's values.

So, to regain the fit between social and organizational values, all of us need to understand how our core values are currently being interpreted and lived out. An organization always reflects, at least to some degree, the society's values because it employs people from the society. Bringing employees together to analyze where those values can actually be seen in an organization's actions is a good beginning to understand how the organization can adapt to a changing society, while still maintaining its foundational principles. When a disconnect occurs, employees and management can work on realigning the organization's policies and practices so that they actually reflect the organization's core values.

The Problem of Changing Technology

Unlike the issue of keeping up with society's changing values and norms, the problem of how to keep up with all the changes in technology seems rather innocuous on the surface. The simple answer is to invest in the technology you need and to train your people to use it. But we don't think that is what most of our respondents are worried about. If we look at the underlying problem with technology, we might reframe the real concern in this way: Given all the choices in technology, which ones will help us become more productive and profitable, how can we afford them, and when do we take the plunge to invest in them? Unfortunately, although these are legitimate questions, they have no straightforward answer, primarily because each organization's needs and capabilities differ.

If we also read between the lines of some of the comments we received, one of the problems related to technology is "workaholism." Technology has freed us to work anywhere, anytime. This has resulted in most of us being less free and having less leisure time, or, at least, we don't spend our leisure time in leisure pursuits. We are addicted to our smartphones and constantly check to see if we have a new voice mail or text message; we log into our e-mail and respond to every "ding" announcing a new one. Even when we are on vacation, we are never "on vacation," are we?

A corollary to this problem is that when we are at work, we are constantly checking technology, too, albeit not necessarily related to our jobs. We surf the Web for new shoes or the latest Fantasy Football rankings; we check-in on Facebook or Foursquare; we send Tweets to our friends and family members; we watch and share the newest, weirdest YouTube video. The bottom line is that we are also caught in a double bind with technology: "Keep up with the latest technology and become proficient at it," and "don't waste your time playing with technology." As Henry David Thoreau said more than a century ago, "Men have become the tools of their tools." It is a sobering thought.

The Problem of Technology-Organization Fit

As technologies become more advanced, there is pressure on organizations to keep up with them, becoming a major problem of fit and, ultimately, just another source of organizational schizophrenia. Consider an example situation in which organizational leaders put pressure on IT to develop or purchase newer, up-to-date systems, but also demand that the current systems' integrity be maintained and kept available to ensure no downtime in productivity. In response the IT department has to create new pathways, protections, and processes so that no one, at any time, is without access to reliable technology. All the while, IT employees keep trying to update and switch to more advanced products and systems. "What," they ask, "is our primary responsibility: innovation or keeping the status quo reliable?" It's a fair question, and one that if it isn't made clear to them ends up causing technology drift—we aren't really up-to-date, but we aren't really able to use the technology we have to do what we need to do.

Another problem with an eroding fit between an organization and its technology has to do with the nature of the tasks or jobs that require information and how the technology provides that information. One notable example has been the complex and expensive technology for manufacturing organizations known as enterprise resource planning (ERP) systems. These are large (sometimes multidivisional) information systems that help schedule production, people, purchases of materials, delivery, and so on in a manufacturing environment. The primary misfit is often between the way the information is processed and provided by the actual system itself (software), the hardware the system is running on, and the information required by the organization's employees and managers. It would be like purchasing a cellphone (the hardware) so that you have handy all the contact information for your friends and family (the information), only to find that the application that runs your contacts (the software) can provide only their first names and the last four digits of their phone numbers.

Not particularly useful, right?

Part of the "how-do-we-keep-up" problem is that an organization's competition may already be keeping up or may even be way ahead in technological advances. But a focus on what everyone else is doing may be a red herring for your organization. In other words, it diverts attention from which technologies are required for your organization.

Theoretically, technology is supposed to provide a competitive advantage when it is used effectively. One of its purposes is to free people from mundane, repetitive tasks so that their skills and abilities are better leveraged for the overall good of the organization. Conversely, technology provides us a time and quality advantage when it helps us do complex, higher-order tasks more quickly and accurately. Additionally, technology should provide faster, more up-to-date information that can be shared more broadly so more people are kept abreast of changes and, therefore, can respond and adapt more quickly and more accurately. And, finally, technology has the capability to connect people across the globe in ways that we have never been able to connect before, resulting in greater collaboration and idea sharing. All four of these aspects should be assessed when an organization is trying to decide which technologies to invest in and where to use them.

Regaining Technological-Organizational Fit

If we look at potential technology from the point of view of the four issues (freedom from repetitive tasks, higher-order or complex tasks, information sharing, and interpersonal connections) we are able to evaluate our technology choices in more structured and relevant ways. First, by asking questions that relate to these four areas, the importance of each can be weighted according to their importance for our particular organization and, even more specifically, for particular jobs and the people in those jobs. Here are some example questions related to just the first of these issues— freeing human capital from mundane and repetitive tasks:

- What types of repetitive tasks do we have in our company, and in which jobs are they located?
- How many of our employees engage in those tasks on a regular basis?
- Are there employees who have skills that are being underused because they are engaged in these low-level, repetitive tasks? If so, which employees and which skills are they?
- If it were possible to purchase technologies that would free them from these repetitive tasks, where would we be able to better use these employees and their skills in our organization?
- Which technologies are available that would accomplish this outcome?
- How much do they cost and, more importantly, what would the return on investment (ROI) be if we purchased them and were able to achieve the required outcomes?

Once you have tangible answers to these questions, you are better able to search for and assess technology in a much more focused and thoughtful way. In other words, these questions provide criteria so that an organization is not just buying technology because it's the "latest and greatest" thing. Rather, technology becomes a strategy for achieving a competitive advantage through better leveraging people's skills in their jobs or throughout the organization, not by merely having the technology itself. The more targeted the technology to help accomplish this outcome, as well as the other two goals concerning information sharing and collaboration, the better the fit between the organization's needs and the technologies used.

As you have progressed through this book, you have likely noticed that the predominant approach we have taken to solve or manage organizational problems is to engage the skills and competencies of the people who work there. By looking at technology through this lens, it becomes clear that rather than fearing technological changes and trying to adapt to them, successful organizations adopt technology to meet the needs of the organization. The benefit of this perspective is that organizations invest only in those technologies that help employees and the overall organization become more efficient, effective, and competitive.

The Problem of Leadership

To accomplish all of the changes required of organizations to become more competitive, to deal with changing laws and regulations, to attract and retain talented employees, and to keep organizations focused on their purpose and vision, organizations must have effective leaders. Unfortunately, the definition of "effective" is somewhat nebulous, particularly when it comes to identifying and developing leaders in our organizations. In this section we address the problem of leadership from the point of view of societal changes that, we believe, have affected our views of leadership. In other words, how do we find and develop leaders who are able to do all that organizations require of them? Our answer may surprise you.

Where Have All the Leaders Gone?

Lee Iacocca asked this question back in 2007,[9] but the question hasn't lost its relevance. We are still asking it about our country and our organizations. The truth is that the answer to this question is simple: They haven't gone anywhere. Rather, they are hiding in the depths of each of us, awaiting our discovery that they are there. Unfortunately, that discovery is usually fraught with fear and anxiety about what others may think of us, as well as our own beliefs that we are not smart enough, savvy enough, charismatic enough, or competent enough to be a leader. As a result, few of us even want to become leaders.

In dealing with the changes discussed in this chapter, as well as with the other persistent problems described throughout the book, organizations must have leaders who understand the problems and who are willing to engage with others to tackle them. We could spend an inordinate amount of time talking about how to select and develop leaders, but that is not our focus here. Rather, we take the position that the goal of any organization is to become what Dr. Margaret Wheatley called, "leader-full."[10] In other words, engaging everyone in the organization in solving and managing the common and persistent problems and challenges will leverage the best ideas and talents of the whole organization. And it will ultimately create an organization that maintains better fit with all four of its environments: regulatory, economic, market, and competitive.

Creating a Leader-Full Organization

Granted, creating a leader-full organization may seem like a daunting task. But it is all in how one looks at it. Wheatley expressed better than we could how organizations should approach this goal:

People are intelligent. We're creative, we're adaptive, we seek order, we seek meaning in our lives. When we really start to understand this, when we really start to change our perception of who people are, then it changes how we think about organizing. . . . There are no isolated individuals in the natural world. Life seeks to affiliate with other life, and as it does that it makes more possibilities available, it makes more diversity possible. . . . It doesn't seek to organize to protect itself, to defend itself—that seems to me a 300-year-old Western conceptual overlay.

I think life seeks systems because systems allow more diversity, they allow individuals to thrive, and they give each of us (when we're in a healthy functioning system) more freedom to experiment with what we want to be as long as we remain conscious of our connections to the whole of the system. . . . Life is self-organizing. It seeks to create patterns, structures, organization, without pre-planned directive leadership.[11]

If we think about what Wheatley said, particularly in taking an HR approach with our five common and persistent problems, we can see that there are two fundamental requirements to creating a leader-full organization. The first concerns how we view employees within our organization. The second is how we discover and create the connections between and among them.

In Western organizations we see employees as individuals; that is, in most organizations employees are seen as separate entities hired and trained to do specific tasks. We evaluate their skills and competencies in relation to those specific tasks, and we often treat each individual employee as if, alone, he or she is can successfully perform them. But, to paraphrase Wheatley, there are no isolated individuals in the organization. We can only know who these individual employees really are, what they can do, or who they can become when they are in collaboration or in community with others. It is a knotty problem for organizations to try to understand individual employees independent of their relationship with others. Therefore, our first challenge in creating a leader-full organization is to look at employees' gifts and talents through the lens of the contributions they make in enhancing and enriching the gifts and talents of others.

For example, consider an organizational project that involves two people. If Frank is good at seeing the big picture, then that talent will complement Joe's ability to see the smaller roadblocks or opportunities within it. Frank will provide a structure in which Joe can make the most of his finer analytic skills. Likewise, Joe's attention to detail will help Frank adjust the overall project view to take into account the smaller requirements and processes. More-over, as Wheatley remarked, "When a group is together it is ca-pable of behaviors that simply are not knowable when you study the individuals. Whole new capacities come forward in us when we are together in our communities."[12] Your job is to be a keen ob-server of those capacities and then to employ them in new and pro-ductive ways. As we mentioned in our discussion of talent in the Chapter 7, moving away from job description or task-based think-ing will also help you with finding the leader in all employees.

In our discussion of strategic planning (Chapter 3) we stressed the fact that planning is a series of interdependent processes that are dynamic and always changing. As with planning, a well-func-tioning organization is an emergent one, reacting to its environ-ment and engaging its resources in their best use. Therefore, the second fundamental requirement for a leader-full organization is to engage employees in all kinds of problem-solving endeavors. As Wheatley wrote,

> Emergent solutions can come from anywhere, but they are always very situational, always highly contextual, and therefore they're going to be quite variable, and always unplanned. . . . Leaders emerge and recede as needed.

Leadership is a series of behaviors rather than a role for heroes.[13]

To engage employees we must first discover their connections to each other. Many of you may be familiar with *Armillaria bulbosa*, a species of mushroom located on 38 acres of forest in Crystal Falls, Michigan. It was discovered in 1992 and is believed to be somewhere between 1,500 and 10,000 years old. The interesting part of this tale is that scientists studied the mushrooms and were perplexed by how they managed to survive all those years, primarily because no one mushroom had the proper structure to survive on its own. Finally, they looked underground and found the answer: *Armillaria bulbosa* is just one large mushroom. It is the world's largest (weighing about 100 tons) and oldest living organism. Its nickname is the "humongous fungus."

And that, really, is what our organizations are—one large organic being—in which no one person can be successful on his or her own. So, the first order of business is to discover all our "hidden" connections so that each person, in conjunction with others, can solve the most pressing problems plaguing our organizations. The second order of business is to create and support an environment in which people not only recognize their connections but are also encouraged to expand them with the specific goal of creating a more leader-full organization.

Sample Solution #5: Dealing with Changes in Your Organization

For our last sample solution, we invite you to create a competition that will be fun *and* productive. Perhaps many of you have seen the reality cooking show on television called *Iron Chef*. The show pits two chefs—one an Iron Chef and one a guest chef challenger—in a timed cooking battle built around a specific theme ingredient. Each chef has a team of sous chefs and assistants and must come up with appetizers, a main course, and a dessert using the specific theme ingredient. Each chef's meal is then judged by a panel of three prominent celebrities and culinary experts.

For your organization, consider putting on an *Iron Chef*-like competition built around one change or challenge facing the organization. You'll want to name your competition something clever, too.

In our sample solution, we will use social media as our theme ingredient. See textbox.

Step 1: First, you will need to introduce a problem or opportunity facing your organization. For our example, let's say that it is something related to marketing your organization, its products, or its services.

Step 2: Invite employees to form teams of four to five people to tackle the marketing issue(s), and tell them that it is a team competition. Once you have described the problem or opportunity as thoroughly as you can, announce that the theme ingredient is social media. Tell them that the ingredient must be a part of each suggestion or idea they come up with. Encourage each team to have its own name or symbol. In essence, the competition challenge is to have each team present a plan to use social media to solve the defined marketing problem or to take advantage of the specific marketing opportunity.

Step 3: Give them a deadline of one or two weeks to develop a plan and create a 15-minute presentation. Set a day for the presentations to be made to a panel of three to five judges, who should be top managers, marketing folks, customers, or whoever you believe is appropriate given the nature of the problem or change. You will need to develop criteria for the judges, such as cost-effectiveness, creativity, widest market reach, or ease of use. Your management team should be able to develop these criteria fairly quickly. The teams should be made aware of the criteria at the beginning of the competition. It would be a good idea to have the teams submit their plans ahead of time to prevent any team from changing its strategies after hearing another team's plans.

Step 4: Invite any and all employees to hear the presentations. Each team should be given about 15 minutes to present to the judges. After all teams have presented, the judges choose a winner and a runner-up. The winning team's plan would then be implemented, and the team coming in second place would be given the opportunity to improve its plan for possible implementation later on.

Step 5: Prizes should be awarded for more than just the winning plan. Consider awarding a prize for "Most Creative Solution," "Most Cost-Effective Solution," and so on, too, to fully reward good ideas.

Concluding Thoughts

"Man who waits for roast duck to fly into mouth must wait very, very long time."

—*Chinese proverb*

By now we hope that it has become clear that your value as a manager or an HR professional in your organization lies in (a) your ability to understand your organization's real problems and their causes, (b) your competency in thinking strategically about how the human capital in your organization can help solve and manage solutions to those problems, and (c) your skills in implementing programs and processes to get the people who work there engaged to do so. These are no small tasks, indeed. But, hopefully, after reading this book, you will be able to come up with your own ways of anticipating and gauging the problems in your organization, as well as coming up with creative, workable approaches to the five common and persistent problems faced by all organizations, large and small.

The sample solutions we provided in each of the previous five chapters are by no means the only approaches you might take.

In fact, we'd like you to think of them more as ideas to jumpstart your own approach to the problems in your organization.

Your challenge now is to begin! As the proverb above implies, no one is going to do it for you—not your boss, not your CEO, not the board, not anyone. The great thing is that you are uniquely qualified to approach organizational problems in a new way, a way that top managers cannot or will not even consider. It isn't their fault, really; they just haven't ever been trained to look at problems from the perspective that they are not alone in having to come up with the solutions. It's a shame, because top managers put a lot of pressure on themselves with this view. And anyone who can take some of that pressure off will be a valuable asset indeed!

The beauty of the approaches you will come up with is that they will work! Why? Because employees want your organization to succeed! By giving each of them a way to help it succeed, they will rise to the occasion with creative solutions and approaches. As an added benefit, they will be more motivated and more productive, because they will see results and they will feel valued as major contributors, not just as replaceable parts. It's a win-win situation for everyone.

Final Thoughts

Are you ready to tackle the five common and persistent business problems in your organization? We hope so. Don't wait to begin, and don't worry about solving everything, because there will always be problems to solve and to manage. As Nelson Mandela said in his book *Long Walk to Freedom,*

> I have discovered the secret that after climbing a great hill, one only finds that there are many more hills to climb. I have taken a moment here to rest, to steal a view of the glorious vista that surrounds me, to look back on the distance I have come. But I can only rest for a moment,

for with freedom comes responsibilities, and I dare not
linger, for my long walk is not ended.[1]

Good luck to all of you who are determined to engage with
employees to tackle the common and persistent problems in your
organization. Together you will be able to climb any hill before
you.

Appendix: Resources and Tips

We wanted to leave you with some additional resources that you can draw on to help you tackle the problems in your own organization. They are arranged by topic so that you can easily find what you need, when you need it. Obviously this isn't an exhaustive list, but we are sure you'll be able to locate some other helpful resources and helpful people along the way.

Some of the resources that follow can be found in articles, books, and on various websites, including the website of the Society for Human Resource Management (SHRM). Some are free, but some require membership or have a nominal associated cost. Some we've created for you. However, if you have a special problem for which you are stumped and none of these provided resources are helpful, feel free to contact either of us for suggestions. We may be able to help you!

Resources for Analyzing Organizational-Environmental Fit

Interestingly, there are not a lot of resources out there for accomplishing a complete analysis. However, a number of resources can assist you in the development of an environmental scan. For example, government agencies such as the U.S. Census Bureau and Bureau of Labor Statistics can assist you with demographic and economic data.[1] Additionally, the University of Washington's Organizational Effectiveness Initiative has a number of resources listed on its website that you may also find useful, both for analysis and planning purposes.[2]

We've provided a grid template to help you organize the leading indicators and your organization's response to them. As your organization requires it, you can add other dimensions. But this will get you started in thinking about which leading indicators you need to pay attention to and about how to help your employees learn to analyze, measure, and report on those leading indicators. Books like Ron Person's *Balanced Scorecards and Operational Dashboards with Microsoft Excel* and Brian E. Becker, Mark A. Huselid, and David Ulrich's *The HR Scorecard* provide helpful tips and tools to organize your indicators and measures, as well as how to embed HR systems as a part of a firm's overall strategy to enhance its performance.[3]

Leading Indicators for an Organization's Environment

Environment	Leading Indicator #1	Leading Indicator #2	Leading Indicator #3	Leading Indicator #4	Leading Indicator #5	Leading Indicator #6	Leading Indicator #7
Regulatory							
Economic							
Market							
Competitive							

Organization's Response to Environmental Leading Indicators

Leading Indicators	Org Response #1	Org Response #2	Org Response #3	Org Response #4	Org Response #5	Org Response #6	Org Response #7
Leading Indicator #1							
Leading Indicator #2							
Leading Indicator #3							
Leading Indicator #4							

Resources for Values, Vision, Mission, and Planning

The Community Tool Box has some great suggestions on how to get started on the entire vision, mission, and strategic planning process.[4] The concepts are easy to read and understand, and the site is particularly helpful for not-for-profits and civic groups, although many of the resources here can apply to any organization.

Most states have one or more Small Business Development Centers (SBDCs) that can also assist you in strategic visioning and planning, particularly if your business is small.[5] Women-owned and minority-owned businesses will also find resources on the Small Business Administration (SBA) website.[6] Your local chamber of commerce can also be a resource for strategic planning, whether through internal means or external referrals.

For some interesting ways to communicate vision and strategy (as well as to engage employees in their development and implementation), Dave Sibbet's book, *Visual Leaders*, will give you some tools and techniques you likely haven't used before.[7] For example, he describes how to conduct visual meetings to achieve greater collaboration, he tells you how to design and manage decision rooms that bring long- and shorter-term decisions together into one context, and he provides guidelines for managing complex projects.

Resources for Market Competitiveness

Because we advocate that regaining or attaining market competitiveness must involve both managers *and* employees, it would be helpful for you to begin by assessing to what extent your organization promotes a learning culture. You might consider doing a brief self-assessment audit to pinpoint where your organization stands at the moment with openness to sharing information. Here are several questions you might start with:

1. Do people at all levels in our organization ask questions and share stories about successes, failures, and what they have learned?
2. Do people take some time following their successes and failures to reflect on what has happened and what may happen in the future?
3. Do managers and organizational systems encourage and reward continuous experimentation?
4. Are people hired and promoted on the basis of their capacity for learning and adapting to new situations?
5. Do performance reviews of both managers and employees include an evaluation of what they have learned and for what they are held accountable?
6. Do reward systems for both managers and employees provide incentives for learning?
7. Do senior managers participate in training sessions and learning opportunities that are provided to employees?
8. Are senior managers willing to openly question and explore their underlying beliefs, values, attitudes, and expectations?
9. Is customer feedback solicited, actively examined, and included in future organizational plans and strategies?

10. Are all managers and employees required to assess and think about their learning quotient, that is, their interest in and capacity for learning new things?

If you answer yes to most of these, you are well on your way to being able to use the full human capital of your organization to gather, assess, evaluate, and act on market competitiveness indicators. If you answer no to some, you will need to put in place ways to encourage people at all levels to adopt them.

A helpful resource for having open and realistic conversations about successes and failures is the U.S. Army's After Action Review (AAR) process.[8] This provides a structured way to have non-blaming conversations about project and process failures (and successes, too) that are primarily intended as learning devices. An online guide is also available.[9] Of course, the military's process is extensive, and you will probably need to modify it to fit your own situation.

Understanding some of the emerging trends in your market can prove insightful. Faith Popcorn—the futurist—has a website that is helpful in understanding what today's consumers and employees are like and what they expect from organizations.[10] If your organization is able to afford it, her future trends consultation may be just the ticket to explore new markets and customers. Also, trendwatching.com has a number of paid and free services for you to explore.[11]

Resources for Legal and Regulatory Compliance

There is probably no better online resource for employment laws and regulations than SHRM.[12] HR professionals turn to this site frequently. In addition, the public policy resources and the specific state law updates on the SHRM website and in the weekly update are also useful. You do not have to be a member to see these, but you will need to be a full member to get advice ("Ask an HR Advisor") or to ask for publications from the HR Knowledge

Center. If you are a non-HR manager, ask your HR professional; it is likely he or she already belongs.

Beyond that, however, there are specific websites and publications that will also be helpful to you, such as the Bureau of Labor Statistics, the Department of Labor, and the Occupational Safety and Health Administration.[13] Your own state probably has some specific state-mandated laws or expected legislative updates on its legislative and department of justice websites, and many cities have regional employers' associations that can help with myriad functions such as salary surveys, research, and training, along with providing employment posters for your organization to post. Additionally, your local SHRM chapter, as well as your SHRM state council, usually offers monthly training programs and periodic legislative updates for its members. Of course, if and when you run into a legal problem, your best resource is always your organization's attorney.

Resources for Attracting and Retaining Top Talent

Like the law resources, SHRM is one of the best places to find the cutting-edge approaches to staffing and retaining employees and senior leaders.[14] There are also some great resources focused on additional approaches to finding talent. For example, you might consider creating a job podcast (aka "jobpod"). With this tool you are able to have job incumbents talk about the ins and outs of their jobs, focusing both on the positive and not-so-positive parts. In essence, a jobpod provides a realistic job preview (RJP) that is credible, primarily because it comes from the person(s) actually doing the job. You can listen to several examples.[15]

There are a number of applications available to create your own jobpod, or you can have your web designer embed or link them to iTunes. However, to see if you might benefit from a jobpod before investing a lot of money, you can try some free ones, like Buzzsprout.[16]

Finding talent, of course, is only the beginning. Those of you who are SHRM members may also find helpful hints and suggestions in the publication *Managing Smart*, which is designed for line and staff managers to help them manage more effectively, thereby helping ensure that the great talent you've managed to find and hire wants to stay. Additionally, the book *Talent on Demand* by Peter Cappelli has some good strategies for developing the talent you already have.[17] Moreover, various LinkedIn Groups have been established to help managers attract top talent, and members can post to the group about the latest job openings and to explain more about their organizations.

Resources for Dealing with Change

There are thousands of resources that tell you how to deal with change. The issue, we believe, is sorting through them all to find ones that will really help you deal with the changes specific to your organization. To that end, here are some ideas that should help you and your top managers, as well as your employees, tackle what needs to be done together as a community.

One of the best books available is John Kotter's *Leading Change*, which was updated in 2012.[18] It's worth a read no matter what type of management position you may hold. To accomplish any change, as we've already noted, the employees themselves must be up-to-date on what the change is, how it will affect them, and what they need to do to make the change successful. Kotter's book lays out the fundamental steps in helping this happen.

Moreover, as a leader in your organization, you need to make sure your messages are consistent (and *not* schizophrenic). If you have decided and communicated the core values of the organization, you need to be able to translate them into actual behaviors. It's important that employees, at the time these values are created, talk through selected scenarios so that they arrive at a consensus of what each value looks like when it is enacted. This is a critical point in translating organizational values into behaviors.

People have to "see" what they are expected to "do." Here is a template that might help you organize this process.

Translating Core Values into Demonstrated Behaviors

Example Core Value #1: **Respect and honor differences**	Example Demonstrated Behavior **Behavior #1: When a difference of opinion occurs, employees ask questions, rather than attack another's view or idea**						
ORGANIZATIONAL CORE VALUES							
Demonstrated Behaviors	**Value #1**	**Value #2**	**Value #3**	**Value #4**	**Value #5**	**Value #6**	**Value #7**
Behavior #1							
Behavior #2							
Behavior #3							

General Book Discussion Group

One of our friends recently told us that she has started a book discussion group for her direct reports. The purpose of this activity is to choose a book that has some ideas or new ways of thinking about issues confronting their organization. Each month they read the book and then meet to talk about the perspectives, challenges, and changes that the author has described. Sometimes the group decides to try out some of the ideas, and a person is assigned to report back the next month on any actions taken and the reactions to the new ideas.

Interestingly, our friend said that a side benefit of this book discussion group is that she is able to learn first-hand how her team sees and thinks about issues and ideas. In that way, when she is implementing a new idea, program, or process she has a much better perspective on how to go about it with her employees. Any insight a manager can have on how employees think and feel about problems and solutions is invaluable in engaging them and establishing trust.

We suggest you might try something similar. You never know what revelations you and your employees will have as you sit together and discuss a book!

Endnotes

Chapter 1

1. James R. Healey and Jayne O'Donnell, "Toyota Executives Not Sure Problems Are Solved," *USA Today*, February 23, 2010.
2. Mark L. Mitchell, "The Impact of External Parties on Brand-Name Capital: The 1982 Tylenol Poisonings and Subsequent Cases," *Economic Inquiry* 27 (1989): 601-618.
3. The term "organization-environment fit" has been used by many management scholars over the past 30 years to determine the most appropriate strategy an organization should adopt.
4. Larry Downes, "Why Best Buy Is Going Out of Business . . . Gradually," *Forbes*, January 2, 2012, http://www.forbes.com/sites/larrydownes/2012/01/02/why-best-buy-is-going-out-of-business-gradually/.
5. Richard Bach, *Running from Safety: An Adventure of the Spirit* (New York: Harper Collins/Morrow, 1994): 245.

Chapter 2

1. Peter Drucker, *Men, Ideas & Politics* (New York: Harper & Row, 1971).
2. Peggy Reynolds, *Call Center Turnover Is at an All-Time High . . . Why? Exploring Call Center Numbers*, 2008, http://cds.cincom.com/?elqPURLPage=26.

3. Nichole V. Crain and W. Mark Crain, *The Impact of Regulatory Costs on Small Firms*, contract no. SBAHQ-08-M-0466 (Washington, DC: SBA Office of Advocacy, 2010), 8, http://www.sba.gov/sites/default/files/The%20Impact%20of%20Regulatory%20Costs%20on%20Small%20Firms%20(Full).pdf.

4. Ibid, 9.

5. Bela L. Musits, "When Big Changes Happen to Small Companies," *Inc.*, August 1994, 27-28.

6. Jeff Bater and Brian Blackstone, "Data Indicate Faltering Demand," *Wall Street Journal*, November 28, 2006, http://online.wsj.com/article/SB122770537038659541.html.

7. U.S. Census Bureau, "Orders for Durable Goods," news release, August 24, 2012, http://www.census.gov/manufacturing/m3/adv/pdf/durgd.pdf.

8. Floyd Norris, "From Miserable to Purgatory," *New York Times*, November 8, 2007, http://economix.blogs.nytimes.com/2007/11/08/from-miserable-to-purgatory/.

9. Personal communication with board members of Goodwill of Northwest Ohio, 2012.

10. George S. Day, "Aligning the Organization with the Market," *MIT Sloan Management Review* 48, no. 1 (2006): 41-49.

11. Philip Hadcroft and Denise Jarratt, "Market Orientation: An Iterative Process of Customer and Market Engagement," *Journal of Business-to-Business Marketing* 14, no. 3 (2007): 21-57.

12. Giovanni Gavetti, Rebecca Henderson, and Simona Giorgi, *Kodak and the Digital Revolution (A)*, (Boston: Harvard Business School Publishing, 2005).

13. Beth Jinks, "Kodak Phasing Out Digital Camera, Picture Frame Division under Bankruptcy," *Bloomberg*, February 9, 2012, http://www.bloomberg.com/news/2012-02-09/kodak-phasing-out-digital-camera-picture-frame-division-under-bankruptcy.html.

14. "Social Media for Business—A Beginners Guide" is available from Epresence Online Marketing at http://www.epresence.ie/services/social-media-marketing/social-media-beginners-guide/.

15. Mary Anne Devanna and Noel Tichy, "Creating the Competitive Organization of the 21st Century: The Boundaryless Corporation," *Human Resource Management* 29, no. 4, (1990): 455-456.

Chapter 3

1. David P. Norton, *Making Strategy Execution a Competitive Advantage*, 2009, a Cognos/Palladium Group study of 143 strategy management professionals conducted by the Balanced Scorecard Collaborative, http://public.dhe.ibm.com/software/data/sw-library/cognos/pdfs/articles/ar_axson_making_strategy_execution_competitive_advantage.pdf.
2. Miguel Pina e Cunha, Patricia Palma, and Nuno Guimarães da Costa, "Fear of Foresight: Knowledge and Ignorance in Organizational Foresight," *Futures* 38, no. 8 (2006): 942-955.
3. James A. Brickley, Clifford W. Smith Jr., and Jerold L. Zimmerman, "Management Fads and Organizational Architecture," *Journal of Applied Corporate Finance* 10, no. 2 (1997): 24-39.
4. See, for example, Henry Mintzberg, "The Design School: Reconsidering the Basic Premises of Strategic Management," *Strategic Management Journal* 11, no. 3 (1990): 176-195.
5. Workamper News, http://www.workamper.com.
6. Dale J. Dwyer and Marilyn L. Fox, "The Relationships between Job Demands and Key Performance Indicators: Moderating Effects of Job Resources in Call Centers," *Journal of Business and Management* 12, no. 2 (2006): 127-145.
7. Dennis Jacobe, "What Matters Most to Banking Customers," *Gallup Business Journal*, January 26, 2012, http://businessjournal.gallup.com/content/152156/matters-banking-customers.aspx#2.
8. The process outlined was adapted from Tom G. Bandy's book, *Moving Off the Map: A Field Guide to Changing the Congregation* (Nashville, TN: Abingdon Press, 1998).

Chapter 4

1. Max H. Bazerman and Margaret A. Neale, "Heuristics in Negotiation: Limitations to Dispute Resolution Effectiveness" in *Negotiation in Organizations*, ed. Max H. Bazerman and Roy J. Lewicki (Beverly Hills, CA: Sage, 1983), 51-67.
2. Thomas C. Leonard, "Origins of the Myth of Social Darwinism: The Ambiguous Legacy of Richard Hofstadter's Social Darwinism in

American Thought," *Journal of Economic Behavior & Organization* 71 (2009): 37-51.

3. Sean Covey, *The 7 Habits of Highly Effective Teens* (New York: Fireside, 1988).

4. George Sacerdote, "How Good Are Your Leading Indicators?" *On Strategy* (white paper series, Sacerdote & Co., Inc., 2002), 3, http://www.sacerdote-co.com/papers/how_good_are_your_leading_indicators.pdf.

5. Ibid, 6.

6. Ibid, 7.

7. Dale J. Dwyer and Morgan N. Arbelo, "The Role of Social Cognition in Downsizing Decisions," *Journal of Managerial Psychology, Special Issue: Applied Psychology's Contribution to Society* 27, no. 4 (2012): 178-192.

8. Monica A. Hemingway and Jeffrey M. Conte, "The Perceived Fairness of Layoff Practices," *Journal of Applied Social Psychology* 33, no. 8 (2003): 1589.

9. Edward L. Glaeser, David Laibson, Jose A. Scheinkman, and Christine L. Soutter, "What Is Social Capital? The Determinants of Trust and Trustworthiness," NBER Working Paper 7216, National Bureau of Economic Research, 1999, http://www.nber.org/papers/w7216.

10. Sim B. Sitkin, Denise M. Rousseau, Ronald S. Burt, and Colin Camerer, "Not So Different After All: A Cross-Discipline View of Trust (Introduction to Special Topic Forum on Trust In and Between Organizations)," *Academy of Management Review* 23, no. 3 (1998): 393-404.

11. John K. Butler Jr., "Toward Understanding and Measuring Conditions of Trust: Evolution of a Conditions of Trust Inventory," *Journal of Management* 17 (1991): 643-663.

12. Triple Pundit: People, Planet, Profit, "The Relationship Between Reputation, Trust and Sustainable Business," http://www.triplepundit.com/2011/07/relationship-between-reputation-trust-sustainable-business.

13. For a complete leader's guide to conducting an after-action review, see Department of Army, *A Leader's Guide to After-Action Reviews*, 1993, http://www.au.af.mil/au/awc/awcgate/army/tc_25-20/tc25-20.pdf.

Chapter 5

1. President Barack Obama in the State of the Union address, January 28, 2014.
2. Arindrajit Dube, T. William Lester, and Michael Reich, "Minimum Wage Effects Across State Borders: Estimates Using Contiguous Counties," Working Paper Series, University of California, Berkeley, Institute for Research on Labor and Employment, 2010, http://escholarship.org/uc/item/86w5m90m.
3. Ibid.
4. *The Dun & Bradstreet Record of Business Closings* 33, no. 1 (New York: Dun & Bradstreet, 1991).
5. Jerold Waltman, Allan McBride, and Nicole Camhout, "Minimum Wage Increased and the Business Failure Rate," *Journal of Economic Issues* 32, no. 1 (1998): 219-223.
6. Boone Management Group, "What Does an Employee Lawsuit Really Cost?" *The Pivot Point Blog*, August 23, 2012, http://boonemanagementgroup.com/2012/08/what-does-an-employee-lawsuit-really-cost/#ixzz2ZhJEOi5q.
7. Ibid.
8. InsurePro, http://www.insurepro.net/html/employment_practices_liability.asp.
9. See the U.S. Supreme Court cases: *Faragher v. Boca Raton*, 524 U.S. 775 (1998) and *Burlington Industries, Inc. v. Ellerth*, 524 U.S. 742 (1998).
10. *Vance v. Ball State University*, 570 U.S. __, 133 S.Ct. 2434 (2013).
11. This statement was retrieved from an insurer's website and may or may not reflect all providers of EPLI, accessed July 21, 2013, http://www.nationwide.com/employment-practices-liability-insurance.jsp.
12. This is the annual survey conducted by Norton, Rose, and Fulbright, LLP and was presented during one of its monthly Fulbright Forums, "8th Annual Litigation Trends Report: What's Trending, What's Not in Dispute?" November 1, 2011, http://www.nortonrosefulbright.com/files/us/images/publications/201111018thAnnualLitigationTrendsReportWhatsTrending3.pdf, retrieved July 21, 2013.

13. Survey conducted by the Henry J. Kaiser Foundation/Health Research & Educational Trust (HRET), *2012 Employer Health Benefits Survey*. Retrieved from http://www.hret.org/reform/projects/employer-health-benefits-annual-survey.shtml.
14. Currently this is scheduled to begin in 2018.
15. We are indebted to our friend, Scott Warwick, JD, for explaining some of the intricacies of the wellness incentives in the PPACA.
16. Phillippa Lally, Cornelia H. M. van Jaarsveld, Henry W. W. Potts, and Jane Wardle, "How Are Habits Formed: Modelling Habit Formation in the Real World," *European Journal of Social Psychology* 40, no. 6 (2010): 998-1009.
17. Nicholas A. Christakis and James H. Fowler, "Social Contagion Theory: Examining Dynamic Social Networks and Human Behavior," *Statistics in Medicine* 32, no. 4 (2013): 556-77.
18. Linda Rhoades and Robert Eisenberger, "Perceived Organizational Support: A Review of the Literature," *Journal of Applied Psychology* 87, no. 4 (2002), 698-714.
19. Albert Bandura, *Social Learning Theory* (Englewood Cliffs, NJ: Prentice Hall, 1977).

Chapter 6

1. Bureau of Labor Statistics, "Employment Projections: 2010-2020 Summary," news release, February 1, 2012, http://www.bls.gov/news.release/ecopro.nr0.htm.
2. Ibid.
3. Ibid.
4. International Center for Peace and Development, *Employment Trends in the 21st Century*, accessed August 28, 2013, http://www.icpd.org/employment/Empltrends21century.htm.
5. Ananya Raihan and Mabroor Mahmood, "Trade Negotiations on Temporary Movement of Natural Persons: A Strategy Paper for Bangladesh," CPD Occasional Paper Series, paper 36, Centre for Policy Dialogue, Dhaka, Bangladesh, 2004, 14, http://www.cpd.org.bd/pub_attach/OP36.pdf.
6. Myrle Croasdale, "Physician Shortage? Push Is on for More Medical Students," *amednews.com*, March 14, 2005, http://www.ama-assn.org/amednews/2005/03/14/prl10314.htm; Bob Miodonski,

"Giant Labor Shortage Needs Educated Solution," *Contractor,*
May 1, 2007, http://www.contractormag.com/articles/newsar-
ticle.cfm?newsid=1149.

7. William O. Brown, Steven B. Frates, Ian S. Rudge, and Richard L.
Tradewell, *The Costs and Benefits of After School Programs: The
Estimated Effects of the After School Education and Safety Program Act of 2002* (Claremont, CA: The Rose Institute of State
and Local Government, Claremont-McKenna College, 2002).

8. Committee on Prospering in the Global Economy of the 21st
Century: An Agenda for American Science and Technology;
Committee on Science, Engineering, and Public Policy Committee on Science; Institute of Medicine; Policy and Global Affairs; National Academy of Sciences; and National Academy of
Engineering, *Rising Above the Gathering Storm: Energizing and
Employing America for a Brighter Economic Future* (Washington, DC: National Academies Press, 2007), http://www.nap.edu/
openbook.php?record_id=11463.

9. To see the complete report on all the behaviors, skills, personal attributes, and competencies identified, see ACT, Inc., *Workplace
Essential Skills: Resources Related to the SCANS Competencies
and Foundation Skills* (presented to the U.S. Department of
Labor, Employment and Training Administration, and the U.S.
Department of Education, National Center for Education Statistics), 2000, http://wdr.doleta.gov/opr/fulltext/00-wes.pdf.

10. The Conference Board, Inc., Partnership for 21st Century Skills,
Corporate Voices for Working Families, and Society for Human
Resources Management, *Are They Really Ready to Work? Em-
ployers' Perspectives on the Basic Knowledge and Applied Skills
of New Entrants to the 21st Century U.S. Workforce* (Washington,
DC: 2006), http://www.p21.org/storage/documents/FINAL_RE-
PORT_PDF09-29-06.pdf.

11. Robert E. Lewis and Robert J. Heckman, "Talent Management:
A Critical Review," *Human Resource Management Review* 16
(2006): 139-154; Chris Ashton and Lynne Morton, "Managing
Talent for Competitive Advantage," Strategic HR Review 4, no.
5 (2005): 28-31.

12. This conceptualization is taken from Lewis and Heckman (2006),
who adapted it from Shoshana Zuboff, *In the Age of the Smart*

Machine: The Future of Work and Power (New York: Basic Books, 1988).

13. Ikujiro Nonaka, Georg von Krogh, and Sven Voelpel, "Organizational Knowledge Creation Theory: Evolutionary Paths and Future Advances," *Organization Studies* 27, no. 8 (2006): 1179-208.

14. Melissa R. Peet, Katherine Walsh, Robin Sober, and Christine S. Rawak, "Generative Knowledge Interviewing: A Method for Knowledge Transfer and Talent Management at the University of Michigan," *International Journal of Educational Advancement* 10, no. 2 (2011): 71-85.

15. Ibid.

16. Ibid.

Chapter 7

1. Alvin Toffler, *Future Shock* (New York: Random House, 1970), 2.

2. Shalom H. Schwartz, "Studying Values: Personal Adventure, Future Directions," *Journal of Cross-Cultural Psychology* 42, no. 3 (2011): 307-19.

3. Shalom H. Schwartz, "Universals in the Content and Structure of Values: Theoretical Advances and Empirical Tests in 20 Countries," in *Advances in Experimental Social Psychology*, ed. Mark P. Zanna (Orlando: Academic Press, 1992), 25:1-65.

4. Shalom H. Schwartz, "Basic Human Values: Theory, Measurement, and Applications," *Revue française de sociologie* 47, no. 4 (2006): 249-288.

5. Milton Rokeach, "Change and Stability in American Value Systems 1968-1971," in *Understanding Human Values: Individual and Societal*, ed. Milton Rokeach (New York: Free Press/Simon and Schuster, 1979), 129-147.

6. In response to Hurricane Sandy, "The IRS provided that employees who donate unused PTO under a program in which the employer contributes the value of the PTO before Jan. 1, 2014, to a Sec. 170(c) charitable organization for the relief of victims of Hurricane Sandy will not be required to recognize compensation income for the value of the donated PTO" (Internal Revenue Service Notice 2012-69). Because the employee does not in-

clude the value of the donated PTO in income, he or she is not allowed to take a charitable contribution deduction.

7. Lindsey A. Owens, "Confidence in Banks, Financial Institutions and Wall Street, 1971-2011," *Public Opinion Quarterly* 76, no. 1 (2011): 142-162.

8. Gregory Bateson, Don D. Jackson, Jay Haley, and John Weakland, "Towards a Theory of Schizophrenia," *System Research and Behavioral Science* 1 (1956): 251-264.

9. Lee Ioccoca, *Where Have All the Leaders Gone?* (New York: Simon and Schuster, 2007).

10. Margaret Wheatley, "The Unplanned Organization: Learning from Nature's Emergent Creativity," *Noetic Sciences Review*, no. 37 (1996), http://www.margaretwheatley.com/articles/unplannedorganization.html.

11. Ibid.

12. Ibid.

13. Ibid.

Chapter 8

1. Nelson R. Mandela, *Long Walk to Freedom: The Autobiography of Nelson Mandela* (Boston: Little, Brown, 1995).

Appendix

1. U.S. Census Bureau, http://www.census.gov; Bureau of Labor Statistics, http://www.bls.gov.

2. University of Washington, Organizational Effectiveness Initiative, "Tools and Templates," https://depts.washington.edu/oei/tools-and-templates.

3. Ron Person, *Balanced Scorecards and Operational Dashboards with Microsoft Excel* (Indianapolis, IN: Wiley, 2013); Brian E. Becker, Mark A. Huselid, and David Ulrich, The HR Scorecard: Linking People, Strategy, and Performance (Boston: Harvard Press, 2001).

4. The Community Tool Box is a free, online resource from the University of Kansas for people working to build healthier communities and bring about social change. It offers thousands of pages

of tips and tools for taking action in communities. See http://ctb. ku.edu/en/table-of-contents.

5. U.S. Small Business Administration, "Local Assistance," http:// www.sba.gov/tools/local-assistance?ms=nid11409.

6. U.S. Small Business Administration, "Women-Owned Small Busi- nesses," http://www.sba.gov/content/women-owned-small-busi- ness-federal-contract-program; "Minority-Owned Businesses," http://www.sba.gov/content/minority-owned-businesses.

7. Dave Sibbet, *Visual Leaders: New Tools for Visioning, Management, and Organizational Change* (New York: Wiley, 2012).

8. The history of the purpose and development of the After Action Review (AAR) can be found at U.S. Army Research Institute, *Foundations of After Action Review Process*, 1999, http://www. dtic.mil/dtic/tr/fulltext/u2/a368651.pdf.

9. U.S. Army Combined Arms Center-Training, *Leader's Guide to After-Action Reviews* (AAR), 2011, http://www.jackson.army.mil/ sites/leaderdevelopment/docs/710.

10. Faith Popcorn's BrainReserve, http://www.faithpopcorn.com.

11. Trendwatching.com, http://www.trendwatching.com. Society for Human Resource Management, "Legal Issues," http://www. shrm.org/LegalIssues/Pages/default.aspx.

12. U.S. Bureau of Labor Statistics, http://www.bls.gov; U.S. Depart- ment of Labor, http://www.dol.gov; U.S. Occupational Safety and Health Administration, "OSHA Law & Regulations," https:// www.osha.gov/law-regs.html.

13. Society for Human Resource Management, http://www.shrm.org.

14. Jobs in Pods, http://jobsinpods.com. Here is an example of a video job podcast from Child Protective Services in New York City that is a great description of what is involved in that type of job: New York City Administration for Children's Services, "Become a Child Protective Specialist," http://www.nyc.gov/html/acs/ html/career/work_cps_video.shtml.

15. Buzzsprout, http://www.buzzsprout.com.

16. Peter Cappelli, *Talent on Demand: Managing Talent in an Age of Uncertainty* (Boston: Harvard Business Press, 2008).

17. John P. Kotter, *Leading Change* (Boston: Harvard Business Re- view Press, 2012).

Index

Figures are indicated by *f*, notes by *n*, and boxes by *b*, respectively.

A

AAR (After-Action Review), 86–87*b*, 189
accountability partners, 117
accountants and accounting, 146–7
accumulated leave programs (paid time off donation programs or PTOs), 160–2
addictions, 109
advertising culture, 147
Affordable Care Act. *See* Patient Protection and Affordable Care Act (PPACA)
After-Action Review (AAR), 86–87b, 189
age discrimination claims, 91
airline deregulation, 23
applicants, 154–5, 168–9
apprenticeships, 124
armed forces, 24, 86b, 189
Armillaria bulbosa (mushroom), 177
association bias, 109
attributes for employment, 127

B

Baby Boom generation, 126
Bach, Richard, *Running from Safety*, 7–8
banks and banking
    customer service training in, 56–57
    employees in, 143–4
    work-family conflict example in, 164–5
Beanie Babies, 30
Becker, Brian E., *The HR Scorecard*, 186
behavioral competency, 152–55
behaviors
    core values and, 192

cultural norms and, 106–7
expectations for employee, 54
health, 110–19
reinforcement for change, 114
rewards for positive changes in, 118–9
social networks' role in, 115
training and coaching for, 109–10
values and, 158
benefits
    children, health benefits for, 96–99
    inequitable, 101
    nonmedical, 104
    organizations' reporting of, 99–100
    surveys regarding, 103
Best Buy, 5–6
Better Business Bureau, 88b
big box electronic retailers, 6
BLS (U.S. Bureau of Labor Statistics), 124–5, 185, 190
book discussion groups, 192–3
breast cancer screenings, 97
Bureau of Labor Statistics (BLS), U.S., 124–5, 185, 190
Burke, Edmund, 89
Bush, President George W., 90
Buzzsprout, 190
buzzwords, 47

C

cafeteria plans, 99
call centers, 19, 55–56
Cappelli, Peter, *Talent on Demand*, 191

Census Bureau, U.S., 185
census data, 147–8
changes
    barriers to, 111–4
    dynamics of, 112b
    in organization (Sample Solution #5),
        177–9
    in organizational health culture,
        116–9
    resources for dealing with, 191–2
    in social norms and values, 158–62
    in technology, 169–70
children, health benefits for, 96–99
China, 126
Chinese proverb, 181
civil rights movement, 159–60
claims
    of discrimination, 91–92
    frivolous, 95
coaching for behavior changes, 109–10
Cognos/Palladium Group, 40
competencies
    behavioral, 152–5
    distrust and, 79–81
    for employment, 127–9, 144–5
    identifying and developing (Sample
        Solution 4), 147–52
    organizational, 148
    validating, 154–5
competition, 65
    between/within organizations, 66
    defined, 66
    direct, 66
    indirect, 67
    market, 68–83
    resource, 67
competitive advantage, 79
competitive fit, 5, 33–37
competitiveness
    attaining, 83–84
    benefits and challenges of, 68–83
    market, 68–83
    resources for, 188–9
compliance, legal and regulatory, 189–90
Conte, Jeffrey M., 80
cooperation, 65
core values
    determining, 58–63, 61b
    translating into demonstrated behav-
        iors, 192
costs
    drivers of, 75–76

labor, 25
Covey, Sean, 71
credit unions, 164–6
critical information
    effect on profitability, 15–16
    examples of, 10–11
    for federal health care requirements,
        101–4
    leading indicators and, 16, 74
    role in market competition, 69–72
    trust and, 81–83
critical problems, distortion and denial of,
    108–10
cultural norms, 106–7
cultural, organizational, 106
culture. See also health culture
    in professions, 147

D

dangerous solutions, 71
demographic changes, 158
dental care coverage, 103
Departments, U.S. See entries at U.S.
deregulation of airlines, 23
Devanna, Mary Anne, 33
direct competition, 66
disability, 91
discrimination claims, 91–92
distrust, competency and, 79–81
diversity
    for accountants and accounting,
        146–7
    in labor force, 126, 136
    in marketing and advertising, 147
doctors, supply of, 141–2
DOL (U.S. Department of Labor), 91, 190
double bind, 163–5, 170
Downes, Larry, 6
downsizing, 46–47, 79–81, 101
Drucker, Peter, Men, Ideas & Politics, 9, 55
Dulles, John Foster, 1
Dun & Bradstreet survey, 90
Dunn, Brian, 5–6
durable goods, 27
dynamics of change, 112b

E

E-ZPass lanes, 141
economic fit, 4, 26–30
economies of scale, 21–22

educational assistance/reimbursement
benefits, 104
emergent approach, 51
Emerging Leaders program, 20
employee benefits. *See* benefits
employees
    career advancement and, 19–20
    in collaboration with others, 176
    development, hiring for, 143
    engaging in corporate vision, 53–54
    engaging in strategic planning and
      implementation, 43–45
    identifying competent current, 148–9
    as individuals, 175
    involvement in current job and
      advancement, 19–20
    realistic preview of jobs for, 19
    supervisor vs. management-level,
      92–93
    supply of, 125–7
    types of, 139–42, 140f
employment
    competencies for, 127–9, 144–5
    minimum wage and, 90
employment practices liability insur-
    ance (EPLI)
    benefits of, 92–94
    costs of, 94–95
enterprise resource planning (ERP), 171
environment. *See* organization-environment
    fit
EPLI. *See* employment practices liability
    insurance
ERP (enterprise resource planning), 171
excise tax, 100
explicit knowledge, 149–50
extension of health benefits for children,
    96–99
eye care coverage, 103

F

Facebook, 31, 85b
facilitators, 60
fads, 30, 47–48
Family and Medical Leave Act (FMLA),
    23–26
family-owned businesses, 55
family-work conflicts, 164–7
FDA (U.S. Food and Drug Administration),
    22, 49
fears. *See also* future shock; uncertainty

of lawsuits, 91–95
organizations' fears regarding laws
    and regulations, 89–121
federal minimum wage, 89–90
fit. *See* specific kinds
fixed pie mindset, 72
FMLA (Family and Medical Leave Act),
    23–26
Food and Drug Administration (FDA), U.S.,
    22, 49
Foursquare, 31, 85b
frivolous claims, 95
future shock, 157

G

Gaines-Ross, Leslie, 83
Gallup Daily Tracking poll, 56
Generations X and Y, 126
Generative Knowledge Interviewing, 149,
    151–2
Glaeser, Edward, 81
GNP (gross national product), 14
goals, realistic, 110
goods, durable, 27
Goodwill Industries, 29
government regulations, 1, 7, 21–22, 89
grid templates, 186–7, 192
grieving and loss, 112
gross national product (GNP), 14
group gatherings, small, 58–62, 85b
group health plans, limits on, 96

H

Harvard University, 115
health behaviors, 110
health care
    children's benefits, 96–99
    federal requirements, critical infor-
      mation for, 101–4
    high-cost employer-sponsored health
      coverage, 100
    hospitalization coverage, 103
    immunizations, coverage for, 97
    penalties for noncompliance in offer-
      ing, 98
    plans for, 96–98
    preexisting health conditions, 96, 101
    preventive care coverage, 97
    providers of, 119, 141–2
    waiting period for coverage, 96

health care organization, work-family conflict example from, 166–7
health care reform debate, 162. *See also* Patient Protection and Affordable Care Act
health culture
 changing behaviors and, 110–19
 changing organizational culture (Sample solution #3), 116–9
 defined, 105–6
 distortion and denial in, 108–10
 information for employees about, 107–8
 norms and, 107, 111–14
 values for healthy lifestyles, 107–8
health problems, 96–97, 107
health risk assessment (HRA), 105
health savings accounts, 99
health screenings, 97, 107
healthy norms, 111–4
Hemingway, Monica A., 80
high-cost employer-sponsored health coverage, 100
hiring for specific jobs, 143
hospitalization coverage, 103
HR Knowledge Center, 189–90
HRA (health risk assessment), 105
human capital. *See also* employees
 in attaining market competitiveness, 84, 188–9
 attracting and retaining, 131, 138–9
 freeing from mundane, repetitive tasks, 172–3
 in organizational problem solving, vii, 2, 181
Hummers, 30
Hurricane Sandy, 161
Huselid, Mark A., *The HR Scorecard*, 186

I

Iacocca, Lee, 174
immunizations, coverage for, 97
indicators. *See* lagging indicators; leading indicators
indirect competition, 67
insurance. *See also* employment practices liability insurance; health care
 liability insurance coverage, 91–92
 providers of, 119
 self-insured plans, 100
insurance company, work-family conflict example in, 166–7

InsurePro, 91–92
Internal Revenue Service (IRS), 29, 97–98
International Center for Peace and Development website, 126
Internet job boards, 130
interviews
 Generative Knowledge Interviews, 149, 151–2
 questions, 168–9
intranet, 130
involuntary turnover, 17
Iron Chef (television show), 118, 177–8
IRS (Internal Revenue Service), 29, 97–98
ISS (company), 22
iTunes, 190

J

Japan, 48
job boards, Internet, 130
job descriptions, 131–3
job podcast, 190
job-person mismatch, 134–5, 145–6
Johnson and Johnson, 4
Just-in-Time approach, 48

K

Kaizen, 48
knowledge
 explicit, 149–50
 Generative Knowledge Interviewing, 149, 151–2
 HR Knowledge Center, 189–90
Kodak, 30–31
Kotter, John, *Leading Change*, 191

L

labor costs, 25
Labor Department, U.S. (DOL), 91, 190
labor movement, 159
Labor Ready, 130
lagging indicators
 defined, 14
 examples of, 35
 in organizational context, 15
 relationship to leading indicators, 17
 resulting from FMLA, 25–26
language and symbolism, 117
laws
 compliance with, 189–90

organizations' fears regarding,
      89–121
organizations' positive adaptation to,
      119–20
stakeholders affected by, 52
workers' compensation, 92
lawsuits, 91–95
leader-full organizations, 174–7
leadership, 173–4
leading indicators
      for an organization's environment,
            186–7
      critical information and, 16, 74
      defined, 16
      examples of, 35
      FMLA as, 25–26
      for market fit, 74–81
      relationship to lagging indicators, 17
      social media and, 85–88b
      and turnover, 17–18
learning agility, 138, 144–5, 152–55
learning orientation, 69–72
      competition and, 78–79
      creating for market information
            (Sample Solution #2), 84–88
legal compliance, resources for, 189–90
legislation, difficulty of organizations adapt-
      ing to, 89–91
liability insurance coverage, 91–92
liability, strict, 92–93
LinkedIn, 31, 191
litigation, cost of, 93–94
logos, 50
loss and grieving, 112
lunch and learn sessions, 117

M

management-level employee versus supervi-
      sor, 92–93
Managing Smart, 191
Mandela, Nelson, *Long Walk to Freedom*,
      182–3
manufacturing occupations, 124
market competitiveness
      attaining, 83–88
      benefits and challenges of, 68–83
      resources for, 188–9
      trust and, 83
market fit, 30–33
      defined, 4
      leading indicators for, 74–81

uncertainty and, 70
market information, creating a learning
      orientation for (Sample Solution #2),
      84–88
marketing, 147
marriage equality movement, 160
MBTI (Myers-Briggs Type Indicator), 43
medical care. *See* health care
metadata, 103
military caregiver leave, 24
military reserve forces, 24
minimum wage, 89–90
miscommunication, 12f
mixed messages, 163–7
mushroom *(Armillaria bulbosa)*, 177
Myers-Briggs Type Indicator (MBTI), 43

N

National Academy of Sciences, 127
National Guard, 24
Newton, Isaac, 111
noncompliance. *See* penalties for
      noncompliance
nonmedical benefits, 104
Nordstrom, 18–19
norms
      cultural, 106–7
      health, 107, 111–14
not-for-profits, 28–29
nurses, supply of, 141

O

Obama, Barack, 90
Obamacare. *See* Patient Protection and Af-
      fordable Care Act
obesity, 115
Occupational Safety and Health Adminis-
      tration (OSHA), U.S., 190
Olympic athletes, 53
organically grown food, 49
organization-environment fit, 4–6
      choosing indicators for, 20–21
      demand vs. supply of workers, 123
      labor supply demand, 124–7
      resources for analyzing, 185–8
organization-person mismatch, 136–9,
      146–7
organization-regulatory fit, 22–26
organization-technology fit, 170–2
organizational competencies, identifying,
      148

Organizational Effectiveness Initiative
website, 186
organizational schizophrenia, 163–7
organizational values, 18–19, 167–9
organizations
competition between/within, 66
fears regarding laws and regulations,
89–121
leader-full, 174–7
as organic beings, 177
OSHA (U.S. Occupational Safety and Health
Administration), 190
outsourcing, 133

P
paid time off donation programs (PTOs),
160–2
Patient Protection and Affordable Care Act
(PPACA)
employers' fears regarding, 100–1
reasons for enacting, 120
requirements of, 95–101
wellness and, 104–5
pay, 25
penalties for noncompliance, 98–101
for noncompliance in offering health
care, 98
in reporting benefits, 99–100
person-job mismatch, 134–5, 145–6
person-organization mismatch, 136–9,
146–7
Person, Ron, *Balanced Scorecards and
Operational Dashboards with Microsoft
Excel*, 186
personal attributes for employment, 127–9
pet rocks, 30
Peter, Laurence J., *The Peter Principle*, 123
Pina e Cunha, Miguel, 42
Pinterest, 31
poll, Gallup Daily Tracking, 56
Popcorn, Faith, 189
population growth, 125
Powell, Colin, 39
PPACA. *See* Patient Protection and Affordable Care Act
preexisting health conditions, 96, 101
premium assistance credits, 97
prescriptive approach, 50
preventive care coverage, 97
private equity investors, 81

problem indicators, 14–20. *See also* lagging
indicators; leading indicators
problems
nature of organizational, 6–7
organizations' approach to solving,
11–14
production occupations, 124
productivity, 25
professional sector jobs, 124
profitability, 15–16
proverb, Chinese, 181
PTOs (paid time off donation programs),
160–2

Q
qualifying exigency leave, 24

R
race discrimination claims, 91
realistic job preview (RJP), 190
regulations, 1, 7
airline deregulation, 23
compliance, legal and regulatory,
189–90
cost of, 21–22
governmental, 1, 7, 21–22, 89
organization-regulatory fit, 22–26
organizations' fears regarding,
89–121
organizations' positive adaption to,
119–20
stakeholders affected by, 52
regulatory fit, 4, 21–26
reinforcement for change, 114
replacement value puzzle, 140f
reserves (military), 24
resource competition, 67
resources
for attracting and retaining top talent, 190–1
for change, 113, 191–2
examples of, 66
for legal compliance, 189–90
for market competitiveness, 188–9
restructuring, 46–47
return on investment (ROI), 172
revenue, 75
RJP (realistic job preview), 190
ROI (return on investment), 172
Roosevelt, Franklin D., 65, 87

S

Sacerdote, George, 77–78
same-sex couples and marriage equality movement, 160
Sample Solutions
#1: Determining Core Values as an Organization, 58–63
#2: Creating a Learning Orientation for Gathering and Using Market Information Expediently, 84–88
#3: Changing the Organizational Culture from "Unhealthy" to "Healthy," 116–9
#4: Identifying and Developing Competencies, 147–52
#5: Dealing with Changes in Your Organization, 177–9
SBA (Small Business Administration), U.S., website, 187
SCANS (U.S. Department of Labor, Secretary's Commission on Achieving Necessary Skills), 127–9
schizophrenia (medical condition), 163
schizophrenia (organizational), 163–7
screenings, health, 97, 107
search engines, 85b
Secretary's Commission on Achieving Necessary Skills (SCANS), U.S. Department of Labor, 127–9
self-insured plans, 100
self-managed teams, 114
September 11, 159
service centers, 77
service sector jobs, 124
sex discrimination claims, 91
Shandwick, Weber, 83
shared vision, information sharing and, 72
ShopGoodwill website, 29
SHRM (Society for Human Resource Management) website, 189
skills for employment, 127–9
Small Business Administration (SBA), U.S., website, 187
small group gatherings, 58–62, 85b
smoking cessation programs, 97, 105, 115
social and organizational values conflicts, 163–7
Social Darwinists, 68
social learning, 115
social media
for market information, 84, 85–88b, 89
in organization media, 178b
sites, 31
Social Media for Business—A Beginners Guide, 32
social movements, 159–60
social networks' role in health behaviors, 115
social norms, changes in, 158–62
societal and organizational values, regaining fit between, 167–9
Society for Human Resource Management (SHRM) website, 189
specificity, 55
stakeholders
communication with, 56
cooperation between management and employees for, 58
downsizing and, 80
market competition and, 69
regulations and laws, effect on, 52
trust and, 83
uncertainty and, 10, 65
Starbucks, 161–2
statistical process control, 114
stories and storytelling, 152–3
strategic planning and implementation
basic problems of, 41–43
conception and implementation, relationship between, 45t
employee engagement in, 43–45
vision, role of, 40–41, 53–57
stress, 60, 69
strict liability, 92–93
success
AAR assessment for, 189
defined, 1–2
lagging indicators and, 14–15
market fit and, 30
role of vision and strategy in, 40–41
skills and competencies for, 128–9
supervisor versus management-level employee, 92–93
supply chain, 70
supply of workers, 123, 125–7
surveys
Dun & Bradstreet, 90
employee benefits, 103
sweeps week, 54–55
symbolism and language, 117

T

tactics, 129
Taft, Governor Robert, 90
talent
        attracting and retaining, 123–55,
            190–1
        defined, 139
        types of, 139–42, 140f
        universality of, 142–3
taxes
        excise tax, 100
        pretax contributions to health sav-
            ings account, 99
team building, 114
team training, 136
teams, self-managed, 114
technical training, 124
technology-organization fit
        problems relating to, 170–2
        regaining, 172
technology, changes in, 169–70
telemarketing departments, 46–47
television, 54–55
templates, grid, 186–7, 192
Thoreau, Henry David, 170
Tichy, Noel, 33
Toffler, Alvin, *Future Shock*, 157
Toll Brothers, 27
Toll, Robert, 27–28
Total Quality Management (TQM), 113–4
Toyota, 3–4
TQM (Total Quality Management), 113–4
trainability, 138
training. *See also entries at* learning
        behaviors, training and coaching for,
            109–10
        customer service training in banks,
            56–57
        teams, 136
        technical, 124
        uncertainty and employee training
            and development, 138
        vocational, 124
trendwatching.com, 189
trust and trustworthiness, 81–83
turnover, 17–19, 137–8
Twitter, 31, 85b
Tylenol, 4

U

U.S. Bureau of Labor Statistics (BLS),
    124–5, 185, 190
U.S. Census Bureau, 185
U.S. Department of Labor (DOL), 91, 190
U.S. Department of Labor, Secretary's Com-
    mission on Achieving Necessary Skills
    (SCANS), 127–9
U.S. Food and Drug Administration (FDA),
    22, 49
U.S. Occupational Safety and Health Ad-
    ministration (OSHA), 190
U.S. Small Business Administration (SBA)
    website, 187
Ulrich, David, *The HR Scorecard*, 186
uncertainty. *See also* fears
        diversity and, 136
        employee training and development
            and, 138
        FMLA and, 24
        information and, 10, 70, 83, 87
        lawsuits and, 95
        market competitiveness and, 65
        market fit and, 70
        trust and, 79–80, 83
University of Washington Organizational
    Effectiveness Initiative website, 186
unlearning, 72–74
utilization reviews, 102–4

V

values
        behaviors and, 158
        changes in, 158–62
        core, 58–63, 61b, 192
        defined, 158
        for healthy lifestyles, 107–8
        organizational, 18–19, 167–9
        replacement value puzzle, 140f
        shaped by experiences, 159–62
        social and organizational conflicts
            in, 163–7
        universal, 158
values frame, 162
Vance v. Ball State University, 92–93
vendors, 158
victim mentality, 7–8
vision
        information sharing and, 72
        roles of, 40–41
        strategy and, 40–41, 53–57

vocational training, 124
voluntary turnover, 17–18

W

waiting period for health coverage, 96
Wall Street Journal, 26
websites
    Faith Popcorn's, 189
    InsurePro, 91
    International Center for Peace and
        Development, 126
    SBA, 187
    ShopGoodwill, 29
    SHRM, 185, 189–90
    state and federal, 190
    trendwatching, 189

University of Washington Organizational
    Effectiveness Initiative, 186
well-baby care coverage, 97
wellness, 104–5
Wheatley, Dr. Margaret, 174–6
work-family conflicts, 164–7
Workampers, 52
workers, supply of, 125–7. *See also*
    employees
workers' compensation laws, 92
World Bank, 126

Y

Yelp, 85*b*

About the Authors

Dr. Dale J. Dwyer joined The University of Toledo faculty in 1989 and is professor of Management and former chair of the Department of Management. He holds a Ph.D. in business administration from the University of Nebraska-Lincoln, and both an M.A. and B.A. in communication from the University of Cincinnati. In 1995, Dwyer received the "University Outstanding Teaching Award," a distinction conferred only once upon a faculty member, as well as the first UT "Student Impact Award" in 2011.

He is the co-author of the top-selling SHRM-published book, *Got a Minute? The 9 Lessons Every HR Professional Must Learn* (2010). He continues to publish in management and HR management journals, and he holds board membership and offices with several professional management and HR management groups and community boards.

Dr. Sheri A. Caldwell received an undergraduate degree in industrial organization psychology from Bowling Green State University. She also received an MBA and a Ph.D. in human resource development from the University of Toledo. Caldwell is currently the HR director in the Grain Group at The Andersons and continues to teach undergraduate through Ph.D.-level HR courses at Lourdes University and Sullivan University.

She is the co-author of the top-selling SHRM-published book, *Got a Minute? The 9 Lessons Every HR Professional Must Learn* (2010). Sheri has her SPHR certification and is a Certified Internet Recruiter as well as certified in EQ-I and EQ-360 for Emotional Intelligence, also the subject of her first book, *Developing Emotional Intelligence In Others* (2009) with Dr. Linda Gravett. She is also on the Board of the Employers' Association and involved with other local HR committees.

Additional SHRM-Published Books

The ACE Advantage: How Smart Companies Unleash Talent for Optimal Performance
William Schiemann

Business-Focused HR: 11 Processes to Drive Results
Scott Mondore, Shane Douthitt, and Marissa Carson

The Chief HR Officer: Defining the New Role of Human Resource Leaders
Patrick Wright, John Boudreau, David Pace, Elizabeth "Libby" Sartain, Paul McKinnon, and Richard Antoine

Employee Surveys That Work: Improving Design, Use, and Organizational Impact
Alec Levenson

Got A Minute? The 9 Lessons Every HR Professional Must Learn to Be Successful
Dale Dwyer and Sheri Caldwell

Healthy Employees, Healthy Business: Easy, Affordable Ways to Promote Workplace Wellness
Ilona Bray

HR at Your Service: Lessons from Benchmark Service Organizations
Gary Latham and Robert Ford

Point Counterpoint: New Perspectives on People & Strategy
Anna Tavis, Richard Vosburgh, and Ed Gubman

Proving the Value of HR: How and Why to Measure ROI
Jack Phillips and Patricia Pulliam Phillips

SHRM Human Capital Benchmarking
Society for Human Resource Management

Stop Bullying at Work: Strategies and Tools for HR and Legal Professionals
Teresa Daniel

Transformational Diversity: Why and How Intercultural Competencies Can Help Organizations to Survive and Thrive
Fiona Citkin and Lynda Spielman